中华人民共和国
外交系列特种纪念封目录

THE PEOPLE'S REPUBLIC OF CHINA
CATALOGUE OF SPECIAL DIPLOMATIC COMMEMORATIVE COVERS

马小玲 主编

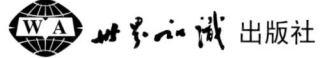

前 言

中国是国际社会的重要一员。中国需要更多地了解世界，世界也需要更多地了解中国。中国外交高举和平、发展、合作、共赢的旗帜，努力践行"以人为本"、"外交为民"的理念，为维护国家的主权、安全和发展利益，保障中国公民的合法权益，增进中国和世界各国人民的相互了解和友好合作，促进世界和平与发展发挥了重要作用，取得了举世瞩目的成就。

邮票是国家的名片，随着信件走遍世界各地。外交部集邮协会与中国集邮总公司1999年起合作发行的外交系列特种纪念封，就是增进中国人民和世界人民相互了解和友谊的使者，是新中国外交成就的历史见证。

外交系列特种纪念封一般在中国与外国建交逢五周年或逢十周年纪念日发行。信封正面贴有中国邮票或中外两国邮票，并以纪念邮戳盖销，信封背面有中文和相关国家文字对照的说明。第一轮建交纪念封以两国国旗为图案，后作为A系列，但在信封上未明确标示。2004年起发行的第二轮建交纪念封，以两国国徽为图案，2006年至2009年作为C系列发行。2009年起发行的第三轮建交纪念封，选取飘扬的国旗等两国代表性事物为图案，内容涉及两国的风土人情等多方面。

为外国国家元首和国际组织领导人来华访问而特别发行的纪念封，也是外交系列纪念封的题材之一；还有一些为纪念重大外交事件特别发行的纪念封，这些纪念建交题材以外的外交纪念封，以及2004、2005年的国徽图案纪念封作为B系列发行，未单独编号。

2010年起，外交系列特种纪念封改为按年度编号发行。

为了使社会各界特别是外交专题集邮者全面了解中国外交系列特种纪念封的发行实况，便于收藏、研究，现将1999年以来外交部集邮协会与中国集邮总公司合作编号发行的外交系列特种纪念封，按系列编号或发行年度为序，分别编制目录（其中一百多种另有特别制作的无邮政编码框的同图国外用封，目录未予收录）。

此外，为我国驻外使领馆举办建交纪念活动而特别制作的外交纪念封（无编号），亦按发行时间先后赋予序号，编入目录，供读者参考。

外交纪念封的发行是一项开创性的工作，且连续十几年，成为系列，在世界外交史上尚无先例，在集邮史上是个突破。外交系列特种纪念封准确地记载了中外两国的国名、国旗、国徽、建交日期。几十种相关国家的文字，反映各国自然、人文特征的邮票和风格迥异的纪念邮戳，寓政治性、艺术性、知识性于一体。外交纪念封被人们争相收藏，成为宝贵的精神财富。

外交系列特种纪念封问世后，在中外领导人参加的纪念中国与外国建交庆祝活动中，外交系列特种纪念封的揭幕仪式渐成惯例。一些外国邮政部门还特别为建交纪念活动发行相关邮票、纪念封等邮品。

外交纪念封的成长，得到了中国集邮总公司，外交部各司局、驻外使领馆等部门的直接指导和各国驻华使馆的大力支持。借此机会，向十五年来为外交纪念封做出贡献的中外朋友，向为本书出版发行给予支持、帮助的各界朋友，表示衷心感谢！

鉴于外交纪念封发行时间延续多年，尽管本目录编辑过程中对资料进行了多次梳理核对，仍可能存在疏漏不妥之处，期待读者不吝指正。

马小玲

2013 年 9 月

Preface

An important part in international community, China needs to know more about the world, and vice versa. China always holds high the banner of peace, development cooperation and mutual benefit, and strives to fulfill the ideal of "People First" and "Diplomacy for the People". Chinese diplomacy has achieved great success in upholding China's sovereignty, security and development interests; safeguarding the legitimate rights and interests of Chinese citizens; enhancing mutual understanding and friendly cooperation between Chinese and people all over the world and promoting the peace and development of the world.

Stamps serve as the name card of a country, traveling around the world with letters and mails. Since 1999, the Philatelic Association of the Ministry of Foreign Affairs and China National Philatelic Corporation have joined hands in issuing several series of special commemorative covers, which are not only envoys for promoting the mutual understanding and friendship between peoples of China and the world, but also the witness to the accomplishments that the People's Republic of China has made in diplomacy.

Basically, the special diplomatic commemorative covers (hereinafter referred to as "DCCs") are issued on the anniversary, every five or ten years since the establishment of diplomatic relations between China and a specific foreign country. Either Chinese stamps or both Chinese and foreign stamps are seen on the front, with commemorative cancelations; while the introductions in both Chinese and the relevant language appear on the back. The first round of DCCs, later regarded as Series A which is not marked on the commemorative covers, adopts the patterns of national flags of both countries as the main design. National emblems of both countries can be seen as the main design on the second round of DCCs starting from 2004, among which the ones from 2006 to 2009 are marked as Series C. The third round of DCCs since 2009 chooses flying national flags and other representative elements in folk customs and cultures of both countries as the main design.

Special commemorative covers, issued to honor the state visits to China by leaders of foreign countries or international organizations, or to mark important diplomatic events, count also as DCCs. With no serial numbers of their won, they have been regarded, together with those issued in 2004 and 2005 with the design of national emblems, as Series B.

Since 2010, the DCCs have been issued according to the respective years.

This collection aims to help understand the big picture of the issuing of DCCs and make it convenient to collect and research. Included in the collection are the DCCs issued since 1999 with joint efforts of the Philatelic Association of the Ministry of Foreign Affairs and China National Philatelic Corporation, complied according to either series numbers or years. (Among all, some 100 pieces of DCCs specially produced without frames for postal codes for international mails are not included in the catalogue.) Additionally, the DCCs (without serial numbers) specially issued to commemorate the diplomatic events held in embassies and consulates of China stationed abroad are included by time order in the catalogue.

A groundbreaking task continuing for more than a decade, the issuing of DCCs has been unprecedented, not only in the history of world diplomacy, but also the history of Chinese philately. Names, national flags, national emblems and dates of the establishment of diplomatic relations of China and other countries are recorded on the DCCs; while the introductions in various languages, as well as the stamps with respective features and distinguished commemorative cancelations, have made the DCCs outstanding carriers in terms of politics, art, and knowledge. Collected always with enthusiasm, they have become precious spiritual wealth.

Since the first diplomatic commemorative cover, the launching ceremony has become a routine on occasions of celebrations for the establishment of diplomatic relations between China and foreign countries. Some foreign postal administrations would also issue stamps, commemorative covers or other philatelic items for the occasions.

The development of DCCs owes its success to the support from China National Philatelic Corporation, departments of the Ministry of Foreign Affairs, embassies and consulates of China stationed abroad, and embassies of foreign countries in China. This book is therefore also dedicated to those who have made contributions to the DCCs in the past fifteen years, and those who have helped publish the book. Thank you!

In consideration of the long time span of these DCCs, omissions or inappropriateness might have survived, in spite of repeated careful compiling and editing. It is with great respect to receive your corrections.

Ma Xiaoling
September 2013

使用说明

一、 本目录收录了外交部集邮协会与中国集邮总公司自1999年1月至2013年12月期间合作发行的外交系列特种纪念封的基本情况。包括中国集邮总公司面向公众发行的编号外交系列特种纪念封281套282枚,外交部及驻外使领馆为举办纪念活动制作的外交纪念封(无编号)61套67枚,共342套349枚。

二、 本目录正文按外交特种纪念封公开发行的系列编号顺序分别排列。1999年至2009年发行的由顺序编号1—179号(含A、B系列共180枚)和C系列1—29号组成。2010年至2013年发行的按年度编号共73枚。

另有2004年至2013年由外交部及驻外使领馆为举办建交纪念活动制作的无编号外交纪念封。为便于整理,以WH-为前缀,按发行时间先后另编序号,共61套67枚。其中54套60枚委托中国集邮总公司制作。7套由我国驻外使馆为举办建交纪念活动与外交部集邮协会临时制作的外交纪念封,目录中均已说明。

三、 本目录对外交系列特种纪念封制作发行的基本情况进行实录。目录内容包括:每套外交纪念封的编号或序号、中英文名称、发行日期、信封正面彩图、贴票、信封规格、设计者和发行量等技术资料。

外交纪念封一般每套1枚,目录中不另标注;少数一套多枚的纪念封,在技术资料中说明。纪念封全套枚数以封图的种类作为确认依据。贴票情况说明纪念封所贴中外邮票的品种差异,同一种封图仅贴票品种不同的纪念封视为一种。纪念邮戳的图文和销票位置以附图为准,不另描述。

中国驻外使领馆或外国驻华使馆为举办建交纪念活动使用的纪念封,有时在公开发行的只贴中国邮票的外交纪念封上再加贴相应国家的邮票,并以该国戳记盖销。此类加贴外国邮票的纪念封不另列序号,在技术资料之后附有加贴外国邮票的外交纪念封彩图。

外交纪念封编印制作中出现的特殊情况,均在技术资料后注明。

四、附录是外交系列特种纪念封的国别索引。按各洲和各国中文国名汉语拼音音序排列，英文国名便于读者使用。索引列出该国与中国建交的时间，以及与该国或国际组织相关的外交纪念封系列编号（或序号），便于在目录的相应系列内查找。

Instruction

1. The catalogue contains basic information of special diplomatic commemorative covers (hereinafter referred to as DCCs) issued from January 1999 to December 2013 by the Philatelic Association of the Ministry of Foreign Affairs and China National Philatelic Corporation (CNPC). There are totally 349 pieces of DCCs in 342 sets: 282 pieces in 281 sets with serial numbers, issued by CNPC to the public; 67 pieces in 61 sets without serial numbers, produced in celebration of the commemorative events of Chinese Ministry of Foreign Affairs and overseas embassies and consulates.

2. The DCCs included are numbered according to their serial numbers: No.1 to No.179 (a total of 180 pieces of Series A and Series B) and No.1 to No.29 of Series C issued from 1999 to 2009; 73 pieces numbered by time order and issued from 2010 to 2013.

Also included are a total of 67 pieces in 61 sets numbered by time order, produced by Chinese Ministry of Foreign Affairs and overseas embassies and consulates from 2004 to 2013 in celebration of commemorative events, prefixed with WH. Among those, 60 pieces in 54 sets were produced by CNPC, and 7 sets by overseas embassies of China and the Philatelic Association of the Ministry of Foreign Affairs.

3. This catalogue serves as a faithful record of the DCCs, covering information of serial numbers, Chinese and English titles, dates of issue, colored designs on the front, stamps, sizes of covers, designers and circulation.

Generally, each set of DCCs contains one piece of commemorative cover only, which is not specially mentioned in the catalogue; information will be given along with the description of the stamps for the few sets that contain more than one piece. Those with the same designs but different stamps are seen as the same kind.

Some of the DCCs produced for commemorative events of overseas embassies of China and foreign embassies in China with only Chinese stamps are sometimes issued with attached stamps and cancelations of relevant countries. Colored illustrations of such kind of DCCs without specific serial numbers can be found after the technical information.

Exceptional cases during the process of the production of DCCs are noted after the technical information.

4. Appendix serves as the index to the countries included in the DCCs. People can search by the Chinese pinyin and English names of the countries, convenient for both Chinese and foreign readers. The index also lists the establishment date of diplomatic relationship and the series number of DCCs accordingly for the convenience of locating.

目 录

1. 外交系列特种纪念封顺序号系列（PFTN·WJ-1—PFTN·WJ-179） ……… 1

2. 外交系列特种纪念封 C 系列（PFTN·WJ(C)-1—PFTN·WJ(C)-29） ……… 103

3. 外交系列特种纪念封年度编号系列（PFTN·WJ2010-1—PFTN·WJ2013-14） …… 119

4. 外交系列特种纪念封（无编号）（WH-1—WH-61） ……………… 179

附录

各国（国际组织）与中华人民共和国建交时间及相关外交系列特种纪念封索引 … 213

后记 ……………………………………………………………………… 223

Catalogue

1. Series in Sequence (PFTN·WJ-1—PFTN·WJ-179) ·················· 1

2. Series C (PFTN·WJ(C)-1—PFTN·WJ(C)-29) ·················· 103

3. Annual Series (PFTN·WJ2010-1—PFTN·WJ2013-14) ·················· 119

4. Commemorative Covers without Serial Numbers (WH-1—WH-61) ·················· 179

Appendix

Dates of the establishment of diplomatic relations between the People's Republic of China and foreign countries (or international organizations) and relevant special diplomatic commemorative covers ·················· 213

1. 外交系列特种纪念封顺序号系列

(PFTN·WJ-1—PFTN·WJ-179)

1999年1月至2009年10月发行

PFTN·WJ-1
中华人民共和国与美利坚合众国建交二十周年纪念封
The 20th Anniversary of the Establishment of Diplomatic Relations between the People's Republic of China and the United States of America — Commemorative Cover
1999年1月1日发行

贴票：1994-15《鹤》2枚
信封规格：208mm×110mm
纪念封、戳设计：马小玲、杨莹
发行量：50 000枚

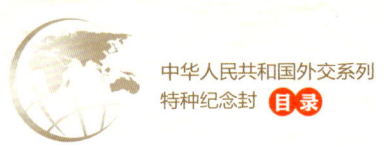

中华人民共和国外交系列
特种纪念封 目录

PFTN·WJ-2
中华人民共和国与法兰西共和国建交三十五周年纪念封
The 35th Anniversary of the Establishment of Diplomatic Relations between the People's Republic of China and the Republic of France — Commemorative Cover
1999年1月27日发行

贴票：1998-20《故宫与卢浮宫》2枚
信封规格：208mm×110mm
纪念封、戳设计：马小玲、杨莹
发行量：50 000枚

PFTN·WJ-3
中华人民共和国与苏丹共和国建交四十周年纪念封
The 40th Anniversary of the Establishment of Diplomatic Relations between the People's Republic of China and the Republic of the Sudan — Commemorative Cover
1999年2月4日发行

贴票：1993-3《野骆驼》2枚
信封规格：208mm×110mm
纪念封、戳设计：马小玲、杨莹
发行量：50 000枚

PFTN·WJ-4
中华人民共和国与葡萄牙共和国建交二十周年纪念封
The 20th Anniversary of the Establishment of Diplomatic Relations between the People's Republic of China and the Portuguese Republic — Commemorative Cover
1999年2月8日发行

贴票：1995-22《联合国成立五十周年》2枚
信封规格：208mm×110mm
纪念封、戳设计：马小玲、杨莹
发行量：50 000枚

PFTN·WJ-5
中华人民共和国与巴林国建交十周年纪念封
The 10th Anniversary of the Establishment of Diplomatic Relations between the People's Republic of China and the Kingdom of Bahrain — Commemorative Cover
1999年4月18日发行

贴票：T149《彩陶》2枚
信封规格：208mm×110mm
纪念封、戳设计：马小玲、杨莹
发行量：50 000枚

中华人民共和国外交系列特种纪念封 目录

PFTN·WJ-6
中华人民共和国与加蓬共和国建交二十五周年纪念封
The 25th Anniversary of the Establishment of Diplomatic Relations between the People's Republic of China and the Gabonese Republic — Commemorative Cover
1999年4月20日发行

贴票：1996-7《苏铁》2枚
信封规格：208mm×110mm
纪念封、戳设计：马小玲、杨莹
发行量：50 000 枚

PFTN·WJ-7
中华人民共和国与坦桑尼亚联合共和国建交三十五周年纪念封
The 35th Anniversary of the Establishment of Diplomatic Relations between the People's Republic of China and the United Republic of Tanzania — Commemorative Cover
1999年4月26日发行

贴票：1995-18《联合国第四次世界妇女大会》2枚
信封规格：208mm×110mm
纪念封、戳设计：马小玲、杨莹
发行量：50 000 枚

PFTN·WJ-8
中华人民共和国与马来西亚建交二十五周年纪念封
The 25th Anniversary of the Establishment of Diplomatic Relations between the People's Republic of China and the Malaysia — Commemorative Cover
1999 年 5 月 31 日发行

贴票：1993-14《中国古代漆器》2 枚
信封规格：208mm×110mm
纪念封、戳设计：马小玲、杨莹
发行量：50 000 枚

PFTN·WJ-9
中华人民共和国与特立尼达和多巴哥共和国建交二十五周年纪念封
The 25th Anniversary of the Establishment of Diplomatic Relations between the People's Republic of China and the Republic of Trinidad and Tobago — Commemorative Cover
1999 年 6 月 20 日发行

贴票：1992-3《杉树》2 枚
信封规格：208mm×110mm
纪念封、戳设计：马小玲、杨莹
发行量：50 000 枚

中华人民共和国外交系列
特种纪念封 目录

PFTN·WJ-10
中华人民共和国与委内瑞拉共和国建交二十五周年纪念封
The 25th Anniversary of the Establishment of Diplomatic Relations between the People's Republic of China and the Republic of Venezuela — Commemorative Cover
1999年6月28日发行

贴票：1992-7《昆虫》2枚
信封规格：208mm×110mm
纪念封、戳设计：马小玲、杨莹
发行量：50 000枚

PFTN·WJ-11
中华人民共和国与巴西联邦共和国建交二十五周年纪念封
The 25th Anniversary of the Establishment of Diplomatic Relations between the People's Republic of China and the Federative Republic of Brazil — Commemorative Cover
1999年8月15日发行

贴票：1997-18《天坛》4种随机贴用2枚
信封规格：208mm×110mm
纪念封、戳设计：马小玲、杨莹
发行量：50 000枚

PFTN·WJ-12
中华人民共和国与俄罗斯联邦建交五十周年纪念封
The 50th Anniversary of the Establishment of Diplomatic Relations between the People's Republic of China and the Russian Federation — Commemorative Cover
1999 年 10 月 2 日发行

贴票：1999-5《马鹿》2 枚
信封规格：208mm×110mm
纪念封、戳设计：马小玲、杨莹
发行量：50 000 枚

PFTN·WJ-13
中华人民共和国与保加利亚共和国建交五十周年纪念封
The 50th Anniversary of the Establishment of Diplomatic Relations between the People's Republic of China and the Republic of Bulgaria — Commemorative Cover
1999 年 10 月 4 日发行

贴票：1992-8《第 25 届奥林匹克运动会》2 枚，或《第 25 届奥林匹克运动会》和 1999-4《1999 昆明世界园艺博览会》各 1 枚。
信封规格：208mm×110mm
纪念封、戳设计：马小玲、杨莹
发行量：50 000 枚

PFTN·WJ-14
中华人民共和国与几内亚共和国建交四十周年纪念封
The 40th Anniversary of the Establishment of Diplomatic Relations between the People's Republic of China and the Republic of Guinea — Commemorative Cover
1999 年 10 月 4 日发行

贴票：1994-5《宜兴紫砂陶》2 枚
信封规格：208mm×110mm
纪念封、戳设计：马小玲、杨莹
发行量：50 000 枚

PFTN·WJ-15
中华人民共和国与罗马尼亚建交五十周年纪念封
The 50th Anniversary of the Establishment of Diplomatic Relations between the People's Republic of China and Romania — Commemorative Cover
1999 年 10 月 5 日发行

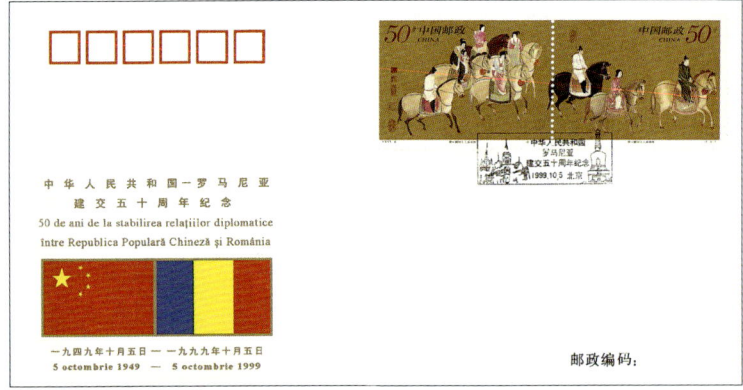

贴票：1995-8《虢国夫人游春图》2 枚
信封规格：208mm×110mm
纪念封、戳设计：马小玲、杨莹
发行量：50 000 枚

PFTN·WJ-16
中华人民共和国与挪威王国建交四十五周年纪念封
The 45th Anniversary of the Establishment of Diplomatic Relations between the People's Republic of China and the Kingdom of Norway— Commemorative Cover
1999 年 10 月 5 日发行

贴票：1998-10《古代书院》2 枚
信封规格：208mm×110mm
纪念封、戳设计：马小玲、杨莹
发行量：50 000 枚

PFTN·WJ-17
中华人民共和国与匈牙利共和国建交五十周年纪念封
The 50th Anniversary of the Establishment of Diplomatic Relations between the People's Republic of China and the Republic of Hungary — Commemorative Cover
1999 年 10 月 6 日发行

贴票：1994-3《鲟》2 枚
信封规格：208mm×110mm
纪念封、戳设计：马小玲、杨莹
发行量：50 000 枚

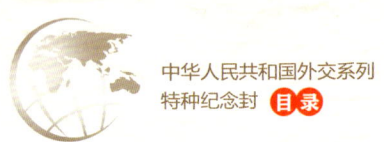

PFTN·WJ-18
中华人民共和国与朝鲜民主主义人民共和国建交五十周年纪念封
The 50th Anniversary of the Establishment of Diplomatic Relations between the People's Republic of China and the Democratic People's Republic of Korea — Commemorative Cover
1999年10月6日发行

贴票：1999-14《庐山和金刚山》2枚
信封规格：208mm×110mm
纪念封、戳设计：马小玲、杨莹
发行量：50 000枚

PFTN·WJ-19
中华人民共和国与捷克共和国建交五十周年纪念封
The 50th Anniversary of the Establishment of Diplomatic Relations between the People's Republic of China and the Czech Republic — Commemorative Cover
1999年10月6日发行

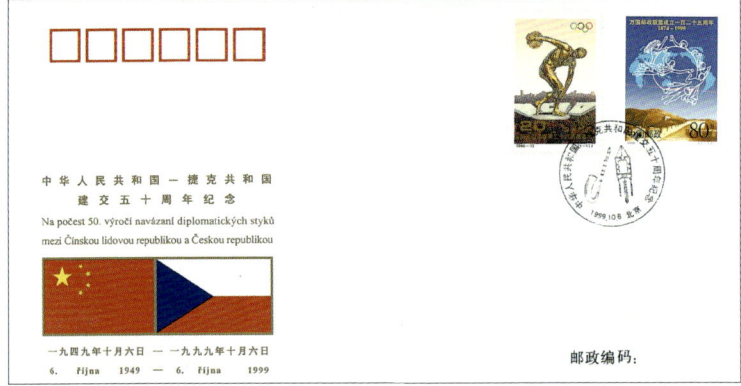

贴票：1996-13《奥运百年暨第26届奥林匹克运动会》和1999-10《万国邮政联盟成立125周年》各1枚
信封规格：208mm×110mm
纪念封、戳设计：马小玲、杨莹
发行量：50 000枚

PFTN·WJ-20
中华人民共和国与斯洛伐克共和国建交五十周年纪念封
The 50th Anniversary of the Establishment of Diplomatic Relations between the People's Republic of China and the Slovak Republic — Commemorative Cover
1999 年 10 月 6 日发行

贴票：1996-30《天津民间彩塑》2 枚
信封规格：208mm×110mm
纪念封、戳设计：马小玲、杨莹
发行量：50 000 枚

PFTN·WJ-21
中华人民共和国与波兰共和国建交五十周年纪念封
The 50th Anniversary of the Establishment of Diplomatic Relations between the People's Republic of China and the Republic of Poland — Commemorative Cover
1999 年 10 月 7 日发行

贴票：1996-3《沈阳故宫》2 枚
信封规格：208mm×110mm
纪念封、戳设计：马小玲、杨莹
发行量：50 000 枚

PFTN·WJ-22
中华人民共和国与蒙古国建交五十周年纪念封
The 50th Anniversary of the Establishment of Diplomatic Relations between the People's Republic of China and Mongolia — Commemorative Cover
1999 年 10 月 16 日发行

贴票：1998-16《锡林郭勒草原》2 枚
信封规格：208mm×110mm
纪念封、戳设计：马小玲、杨莹
发行量：50000 枚

PFTN·WJ-23
中华人民共和国与赞比亚共和国建交三十五周年纪念封
The 35th Anniversary of the Establishment of Diplomatic Relations between the People's Republic of China and the Republic of Zambia — Commemorative Cover
1999 年 10 月 29 日发行

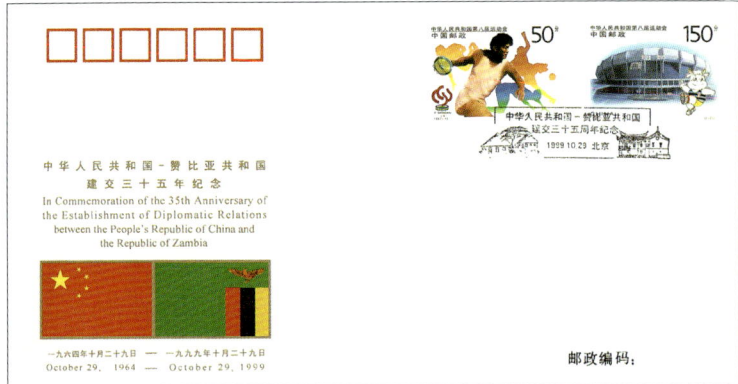

贴票：1997-15《中华人民共和国第八届运动会》2 枚，或 1997-22《1996 年中国钢产量突破一亿吨》2 枚。
信封规格：208mm×110mm
纪念封、戳设计：马小玲、杨莹
发行量：50 000 枚

PFTN·WJ-24
中华人民共和国与阿拉伯联合酋长国建交十五周年纪念封
The 15th Anniversary of the Establishment of Diplomatic Relations between the People's Republic of China and the United Arab Emirates — Commemorative Cover
1999年11月1日发行

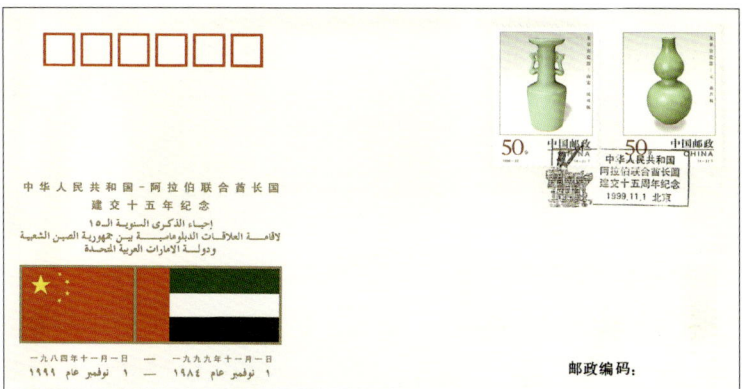

贴票：1998-22《中国陶瓷—龙泉窑瓷器》2枚
信封规格：208mm×110mm
纪念封、戳设计：马小玲、杨莹
发行量：50 000枚

PFTN·WJ-25
中华人民共和国与阿尔巴尼亚共和国建交五十周年纪念封
The 50th Anniversary of the Establishment of Diplomatic Relations between the People's Republic of China and the Republic of Albania — Commemorative Cover
1999年11月23日发行

贴票：1994-12《武陵源》2枚
信封规格：208mm×110mm
纪念封、戳设计：马小玲、杨莹
发行量：50 000枚

PFTN·WJ-26
中华人民共和国与厄瓜多尔共和国建交二十周年纪念封
The 20th Anniversary of the Establishment of Diplomatic Relations between the People's Republic of China and the Republic of Ecuador — Commemorative Cover
2000年1月2日发行

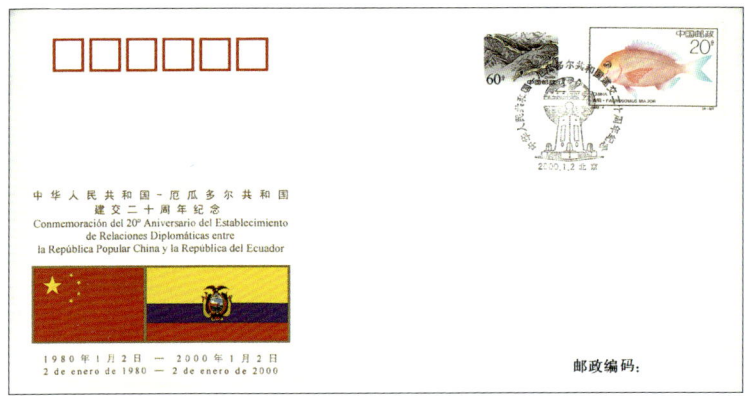

贴票：1992-4《近海养殖》20分和普29《万里长城（明）》60分
信封规格：208mm×110mm
纪念封、戳设计：马小玲、杨莹
发行量：50 000枚

附：加贴厄瓜多尔邮票（2种随机贴用）纪念活动用封

PFTN·WJ-27
中华人民共和国与博茨瓦纳共和国建交二十五周年纪念封
The 25th Anniversary of the Establishment of Diplomatic Relations between the People's Republic of China and the Republic of Botswana — Commemorative Cover
2000年1月6日发行

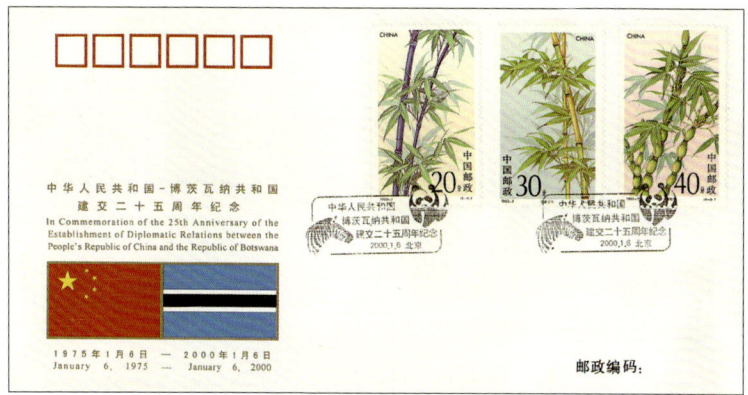

贴票：1993-7《竹子》1枚或3枚拼贴
信封规格：208mm×110mm
纪念封、戳设计：马小玲、杨莹
发行量：50 000枚

PFTN·WJ-28
中华人民共和国与越南社会主义共和国建交五十周年纪念封
The 50th Anniversary of the Establishment of Diplomatic Relations between the People's Republic of China and the Socialist Republic of Viet Nam — Commemorative Cover
2000年1月18日发行

贴票：1997-16《黄山》邮票8种、越南邮票2种随机贴用。
信封规格：208mm×110mm
纪念封、戳设计：马小玲、杨莹
发行量：50 000枚

PFTN·WJ-29

中华人民共和国与哥伦比亚共和国建交二十周年纪念封
The 20th Anniversary of the Establishment of Diplomatic Relations between the People's Republic of China and the Republic of Columbia — Commemorative Cover
2000年2月7日发行

贴票：1997-5《茶》2枚
信封规格：208mm×110mm
纪念封、戳设计：马小玲、杨莹
发行量：50 000枚

附：加贴哥伦比亚邮票（10种随机贴用）纪念活动用封

PFTN·WJ-30
中华人民共和国与纳米比亚共和国建交十周年纪念封
The 10th Anniversary of the Establishment of Diplomatic Relations between the People's Republic of China and the Republic of Namibia — Commemorative Cover
2000 年 3 月 22 日发行

贴票：1992-3《杉树》1 种。纳米比亚邮票 1 种。
信封规格：208mm×110mm
纪念封、戳设计：马小玲、杨莹
纳米比亚纪念戳设计：玛丽·简·福尔科曼
发行量：50 000 枚

PFTN·WJ-31
中华人民共和国与印度共和国建交五十周年纪念封
The 50th Anniversary of the Establishment of Diplomatic Relations between the People's Republic of China and the Republic of India — Commemorative Cover
2000 年 4 月 1 日发行

贴票：2000-4《龙（文物）》4 种随机贴用。印度邮票 1 种。
信封规格：208mm×110mm
纪念封、戳设计：马小玲、杨莹
发行量：50 000 枚

PFTN·WJ-32
中华人民共和国与印度尼西亚共和国建交五十周年纪念封
The 50th Anniversary of the Establishment of Diplomatic Relations between the People's Republic of China and the Republic of Indonesia — Commemorative Cover
2000年4月13日发行

贴票：2000-2《春节》1种。印度尼西亚邮票1种。
信封规格：208mm×110mm
纪念封、戳设计：马小玲、杨莹
发行量：50 000 枚

PFTN·WJ-33
中华人民共和国与津巴布韦共和国建交二十周年纪念封
The 20th Anniversary of the Establishment of Diplomatic Relations between the People's Republic of China and the Republic of Zimbabwe — Commemorative Cover
2000年4月18日发行

贴票：2000-7《长江公路大桥》3种、津巴布韦邮票2种随机贴用。
信封规格：208mm×110mm
纪念封、戳设计：马小玲、杨莹
发行量：50 000 枚

PFTN·WJ-34
中华人民共和国与瑞典王国建交五十周年纪念封
The 50th Anniversary of the Establishment of Diplomatic Relations between the People's Republic of China and the Kingdom of Sweden— Commemorative Cover
2000 年 5 月 9 日发行

贴票：2000-1《庚辰年》1 种。瑞典邮票 2 种随机贴用。
信封规格：208mm×110mm
纪念封、戳设计：马小玲
发行量：50 000 枚

PFTN·WJ-35
中华人民共和国与丹麦王国建交五十周年纪念封
The 50th Anniversary of the Establishment of Diplomatic Relations between the People's Republic of China and the Kingdom of Denmark — Commemorative Cover
2000 年 5 月 11 日发行

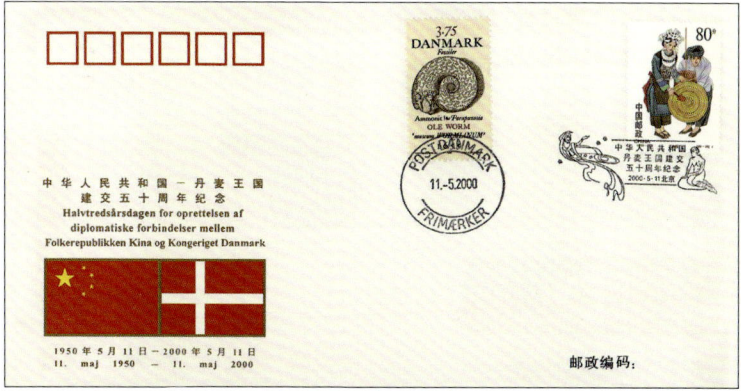

贴票：1999-11《中华人民共和国成立 50 周年—民族大团结》56 种、丹麦邮票 2 种随机贴用。
信封规格：208mm×110mm
纪念封、戳设计：马小玲
发行量：50 000 枚

PFTN·WJ-36
中华人民共和国与缅甸联邦建交五十周年纪念封
The 50th Anniversary of the Establishment of Diplomatic Relations between the People's Republic of China and the Republic of the Union of Myanmar— Commemorative Cover
2000年6月8日发行

贴票：2000-8《大理风光》3种、缅甸邮票6种随机贴用。
信封规格：208mm×110mm
纪念封、戳设计：马小玲
发行量：50 000枚

PFTN·WJ-37
中华人民共和国与菲律宾共和国建交二十五周年纪念封
The 25th Anniversary of the Establishment of Diplomatic Relations between the People's Republic of China and the Republic of the Philippines — Commemorative Cover
2000年6月9日发行

贴票：2000-11《世纪交替 千年更始—21世纪展望》3种、菲律宾邮票5种随机贴用。
信封规格：208mm×110mm
纪念封、戳设计：马小玲
发行量：50 000枚

PFTN·WJ-38
中华人民共和国与莫桑比克共和国建交二十五周年纪念封
The 25th Anniversary of the Establishment of Diplomatic Relations between the People's Republic of China and the Republic of Mozambique — Commemorative Cover
2000 年 6 月 25 日发行

贴票：2000-6《木兰从军》4 种，或 2000-11《世纪交替 千年更始—21 世纪展望》3 种随机贴用。
信封规格：208mm×110mm
纪念封、戳设计：马小玲
发行量：50 000 枚

PFTN·WJ-39
中华人民共和国与基里巴斯共和国建交二十周年纪念封
The 20th Anniversary of the Establishment of Diplomatic Relations between the People's Republic of China and the Republic of Kiribati — Commemorative Cover
2000 年 6 月 25 日发行

贴票：1998-29《海底世界·珊瑚礁观赏鱼》8 种随机贴用
信封规格：208mm×110mm
纪念封、戳设计：马小玲
发行量：50 000 枚

中华人民共和国外交系列
特种纪念封 目录

附：加贴基里巴斯邮票的纪念活动用封

PFTN·WJ-40
中华人民共和国与泰王国建交二十五周年纪念封
The 25th Anniversary of the Establishment of Diplomatic Relations between the People's Republic of China and the Kingdom of Thailand — Commemorative Cover
2000年7月1日发行

贴票：1993-13《龙门石窟》1枚或2枚拼贴。泰国邮票3种随机贴用。
信封规格：208mm×110mm
纪念封、戳设计：马小玲
泰王国纪念戳设计：威娜·占他娜塔
发行量：50 000枚

PFTN·WJ-41
中华人民共和国与加纳共和国建交四十周年纪念封
The 40th Anniversary of the Establishment of Diplomatic Relations between the People's Republic of China and the Republic of Ghana — Commemorative Cover
2000 年 7 月 5 日发行

贴票：1994-5《宜兴紫砂陶》1 种。加纳邮票多种随机贴用，6 种邮戳盖销。
信封规格：208mm×110mm
纪念封、戳设计：马小玲
玻利维亚纪念戳设计：奥尔兰多
发行量：50 000 枚

PFTN·WJ-42
中华人民共和国与玻利维亚共和国建交十五周年纪念封
The 15th Anniversary of the Establishment of Diplomatic Relations between the People's Republic of China and the Multinational States of Bolivia — Commemorative Cover
2000 年 7 月 9 日发行

贴票：1996-19《天山天池》1 枚或 2 枚拼贴。玻利维亚邮票 1 种。
信封规格：208mm×110mm
纪念封、戳设计：马小玲
玻利维亚纪念戳设计：奥尔兰多·塔里法
发行量：50 000 枚

PFTN·WJ-43
中华人民共和国与毛里塔尼亚伊斯兰共和国建交三十五周年纪念封
The 35th Anniversary of the Establishment of Diplomatic Relations between the People's Republic of China and the Islamic Republic of Mauritania — Commemorative Cover
2000年7月19日发行

贴票：1993-3《野骆驼》1枚。毛里塔尼亚邮票3种随机贴用，销票邮戳2种。
信封规格：208mm×110mm
纪念封、戳设计：马小玲
发行量：50 000枚

PFTN·WJ-44
中华人民共和国与沙特阿拉伯王国建交十周年纪念封
The 10th Anniversary of the Establishment of Diplomatic Relations between the People's Republic of China and the Kingdom of Saudi Arabia — Commemorative Cover
2000年7月21日发行

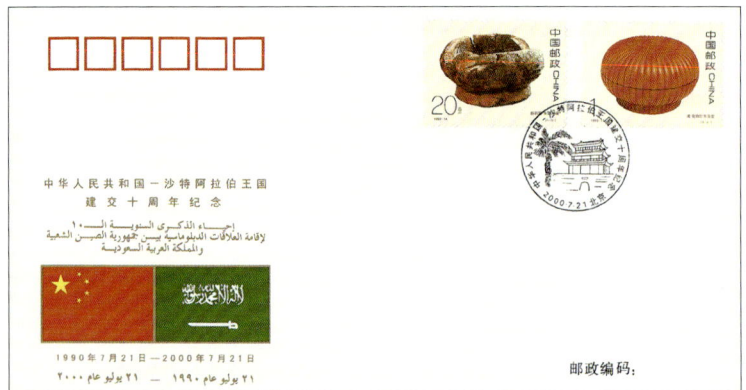

贴票：1993-14《中国古代漆器》2枚
信封规格：208mm×110mm
纪念封、戳设计：马小玲
发行量：50 000枚

附：加贴沙特阿拉伯邮票的纪念活动用封

PFTN·WJ-45
中华人民共和国与尼泊尔王国建交四十五周年纪念封
The 45th Anniversary of the Establishment of Diplomatic Relations between the People's Republic of China and the Kingdom of Nepal — Commemorative Cover
2000 年 8 月 1 日发行

贴票：2000-9《塔尔寺》3 种、尼泊尔邮票 3 种随机贴用。
信封规格：208mm×110mm
纪念封、戳设计：马小玲
发行量：50 000 枚

中华人民共和国外交系列
特种纪念封 目录

PFTN·WJ-46
中华人民共和国与瑞士联邦建交五十周年纪念封
The 50th Anniversary of the Establishment of Diplomatic Relations between the People's Republic of China and the Swiss Confederation — Commemorative Cover
2000年9月14日发行

贴票：1998-26《瘦西湖与莱芒湖》1枚和1994-12《武陵源》1枚。瑞士邮票1种。
信封规格：208mm×110mm
纪念封、戳设计：马小玲
发行量：50 000枚

PFTN·WJ-47
中华人民共和国与列支敦士登公国建交五十周年纪念封
The 50th Anniversary of the Establishment of Diplomatic Relations between the People's Republic of China and the Principality of Liechtenstein — Commemorative Cover
2000年9月14日发行

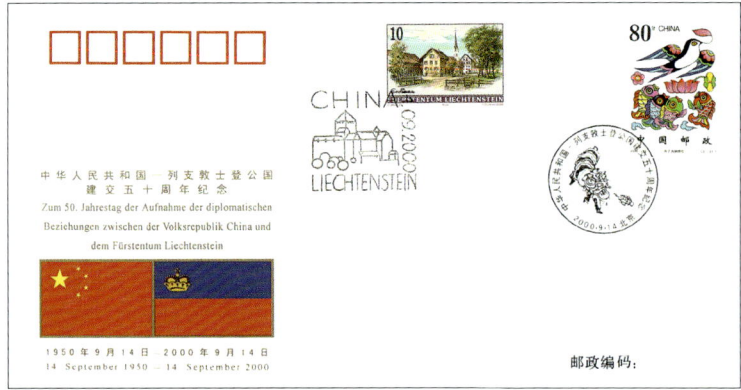

贴票：2000-15《小鲤鱼跳龙门》5种随机贴用。列支敦士登邮票1种。
信封规格：208mm×110mm
纪念封、戳设计：马小玲
发行量：50 000枚

PFTN·WJ-48

中华人民共和国与古巴共和国建交四十周年纪念封
The 40th Anniversary of the Establishment of Diplomatic Relations between the People's Republic of China and the Republic of Cuba — Commemorative Cover
2000年9月28日发行

贴票：2000-18《海滨风光》2种、古巴邮票2种随机贴用。
信封规格：208mm×110mm
纪念封、戳设计：马小玲
发行量：50 000枚

PFTN·WJ-49

中华人民共和国与新加坡共和国建交十周年纪念封
The 10th Anniversary of the Establishment of Diplomatic Relations between the People's Republic of China and the Republic of Singapore — Commemorative Cover
2000年10月3日发行

贴票：1996-28《城市风光》1种或J162《孔子》1种。新加坡邮票1种。
信封规格：208mm×110mm
纪念封、戳设计：马小玲
发行量：50 000枚

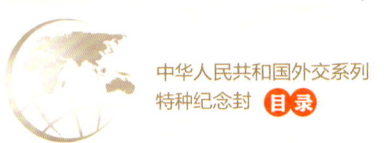

PFTN·WJ-50
中华人民共和国与孟加拉人民共和国建交二十五周年纪念封
The 25th Anniversary of the Establishment of Diplomatic Relations between the People's Republic of China and the People's Republic of Bangladesh — Commemorative Cover
2000年10月4日发行

贴票：2000-18《深圳经济特区建设》4种、孟加拉国邮票2种随机贴用。
信封规格：208mm×110mm
纪念封、戳设计：马小玲
发行量：50 000枚

PFTN·WJ-51
中华人民共和国与加拿大建交三十周年纪念封
The 30th Anniversary of the Establishment of Diplomatic Relations between the People's Republic of China and Canada — Commemorative Cover
2000年10月13日发行

贴票：2000-1《庚辰年》1枚。加拿大邮票3种随机贴用。
信封规格：208mm×110mm
纪念封、戳设计：马小玲
发行量：50 000枚

PFTN·WJ-52
中华人民共和国与马里共和国建交四十周年纪念封
The 40th Anniversary of the Establishment of Diplomatic Relations between the People's Republic of China and the Republic of Mali — Commemorative Cover
2000 年 10 月 25 日发行

贴票：1999-14《傅抱石作品选》3 枚拼贴
信封规格：208mm×110mm
纪念封、戳设计：马小玲
发行量：50 000 枚

PFTN·WJ-53
中华人民共和国与芬兰共和国建交五十周年纪念封
The 50th Anniversary of the Establishment of Diplomatic Relations between the People's Republic of China and the Republic of Finland — Commemorative Cover
2000 年 10 月 28 日发行

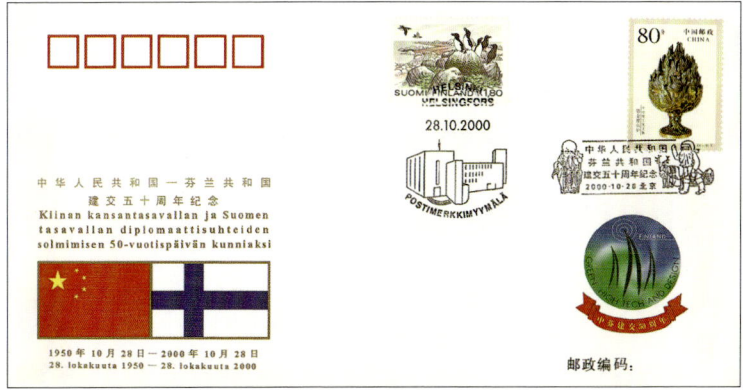

贴票：2000-21《中山靖王墓文物》3 种随机贴用。芬兰邮票 1 种。
信封规格：208mm×110mm
纪念封、戳设计：马小玲
发行量：50 000 枚
注：封面印有芬兰方面设计的纪念标志。

PFTN·WJ-54
中华人民共和国与斐济群岛共和国建交二十五周年纪念封
The 25th Anniversary of the Establishment of Diplomatic Relations between the People's Republic of China and the Republic of Fiji — Commemorative Cover
2000年11月5日发行

贴票：1998-17《镜泊湖》4种随机贴用连票2枚
信封规格：208mm×110mm
纪念封、戳设计：马小玲
发行量：50 000枚

附：2000-15《小鲤鱼跳龙门》5种随机贴用，加贴斐济邮票（2种随机贴用）纪念活动用封

30

PFTN·WJ-55
中华人民共和国与意大利共和国建交三十周年纪念封
The 30th Anniversary of the Establishment of Diplomatic Relations between the People's Republic of China and the Republic of Italy — Commemorative Cover
2000 年 11 月 6 日发行

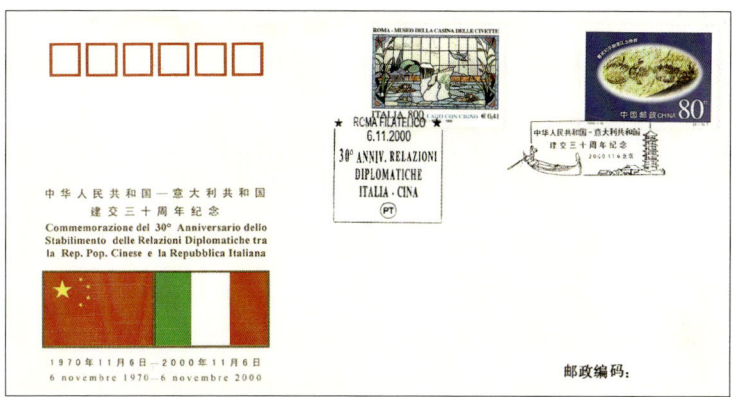

贴票：1999-16《科技成果》4 种随机贴用。意大利邮票 1 种。
信封规格：208mm×110mm
纪念封、戳设计：马小玲
发行量：50 000 枚

PFTN·WJ-56
中华人民共和国与萨摩亚独立国建交二十五周年纪念封
The 25th Anniversary of the Establishment of Diplomatic Relations between the People's Republic of China and the Independent State of Samoa — Commemorative Cover
2000 年 11 月 6 日发行

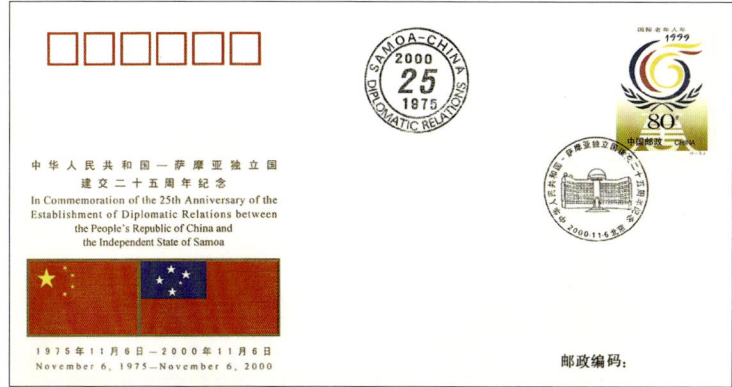

贴票：1999-6《普陀秀色》1 枚或 1999-12《国际老人年》1 枚
信封规格：208mm×110mm
纪念封、戳设计：马小玲
发行量：50 000 枚

附：加贴萨摩亚邮票（2 种随机贴用）纪念活动用封

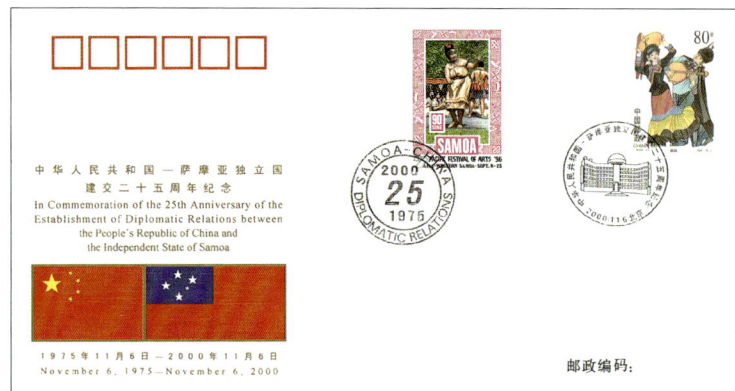

PFTN·WJ-57
中华人民共和国与埃塞俄比亚联邦民主共和国建交三十周年纪念封
The 30th Anniversary of the Establishment of Diplomatic Relations between the People's Republic of China and the Federal Democratic Republic of Ethiopia — Commemorative Cover
2000 年 11 月 24 日发行

贴票：2000-23《气象成就》3 种随机贴用。埃塞俄比亚邮票 1 种。
信封规格：208mm×110mm
纪念封、戳设计：马小玲
发行量：50 000 枚

PFTN·WJ-58
中华人民共和国与智利共和国建交三十周年纪念封
The 30th Anniversary of the Establishment of Diplomatic Relations between the People's Republic of China and Republic of Chile — Commemorative Cover
2000年12月15日发行

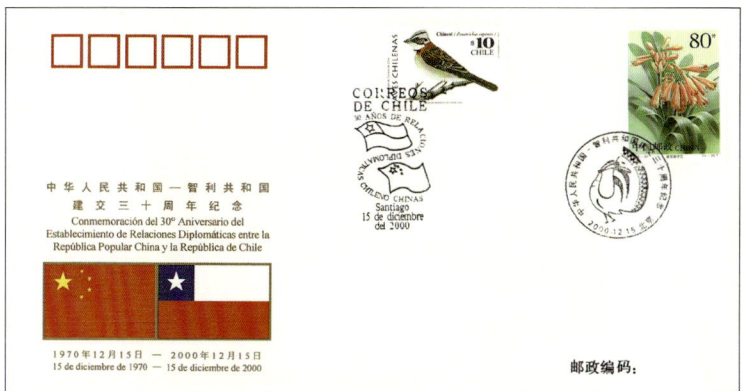

贴票：2000-24《君子兰》3 种、智利邮票 3 种随机贴用。
信封规格：208mm×110mm
纪念封、戳设计：马小玲
发行量：50 000 枚

PFTN·WJ-59
中华人民共和国与尼日利亚联邦共和国建交三十周年纪念封
The 30th Anniversary of the Establishment of Diplomatic Relations between the People's Republic of China and the Federal Republic of Nigeria — Commemorative Cover
2001年2月10日发行

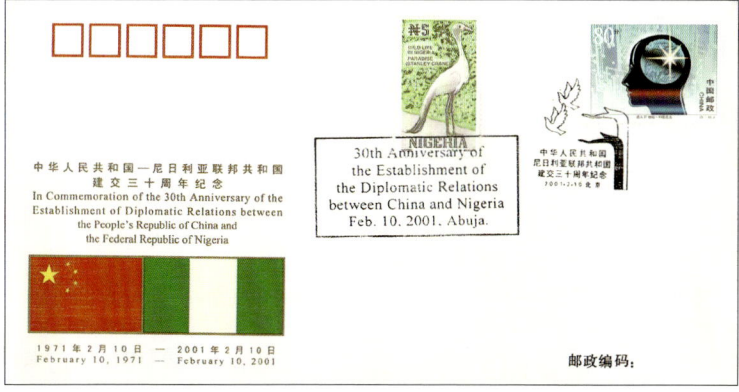

贴票：2001-1《世纪交替 千年更始—迈入21世纪》3 种随机贴用。尼日利亚邮票 1 种。
信封规格：208mm×110mm
纪念封、戳设计：马小玲
发行量：50 000 枚

PFTN·WJ-60
中华人民共和国与科威特国建交三十周年纪念封
The 30th Anniversary of the Establishment of Diplomatic Relations between the People's Republic of China and the State of Kuwait — Commemorative Cover
2001年3月22日发行

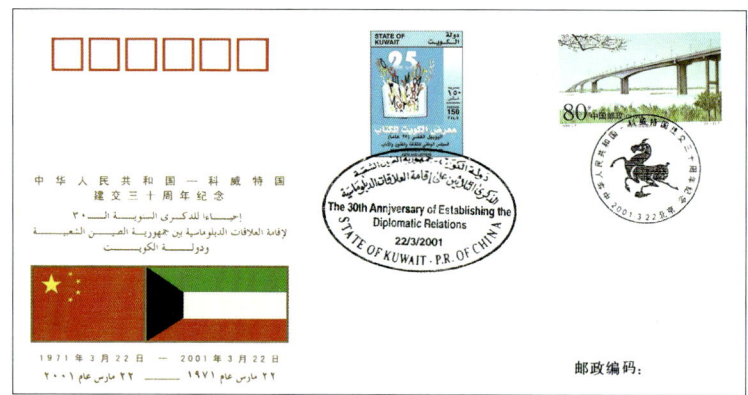

贴票：2000-7《长江公路大桥》3种、科威特邮票3种随机贴用。
信封规格：208mm×110mm
纪念封、戳设计：马小玲
发行量：50 000枚

PFTN·WJ-61
中华人民共和国与喀麦隆共和国建交三十周年纪念封
The 30th Anniversary of the Establishment of Diplomatic Relations between the People's Republic of China and the Republic of Cameroon — Commemorative Cover
2001年3月26日发行

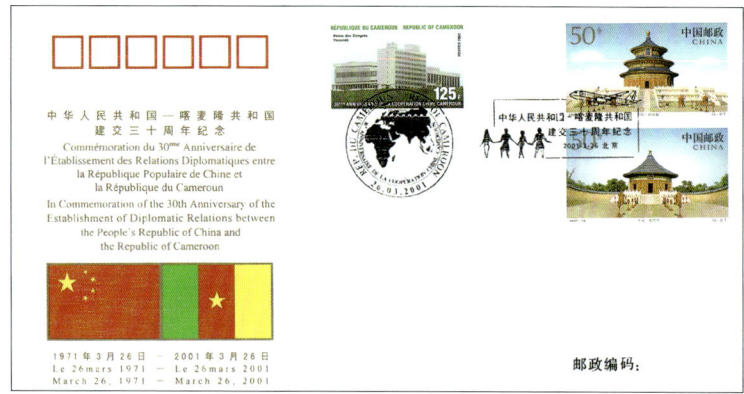

贴票：1997-18《天坛》2枚。喀麦隆邮票2种随机贴用。
信封规格：208mm×110mm
纪念封、戳设计：马小玲
发行量：50 000枚

PFTN·WJ-62
中华人民共和国与老挝人民民主共和国建交四十周年纪念封
The 40th Anniversary of the Establishment of Diplomatic Relations between the People's Republic of China and the Lao People's Democratic Republic — Commemorative Cover
2001 年 4 月 25 日发行

贴票：2001-2《辛巳年》1 种。老挝邮票 1 种。
信封规格：208mm×110mm
纪念封、戳设计：马小玲
发行量：50 000 枚

PFTN·WJ-63
中华人民共和国与佛得角共和国建交二十五周年纪念封
The 25th Anniversary of the Establishment of Diplomatic Relations between the People's Republic of China and the Republic of Cape Verde — Commemorative Cover
2001 年 4 月 25 日发行

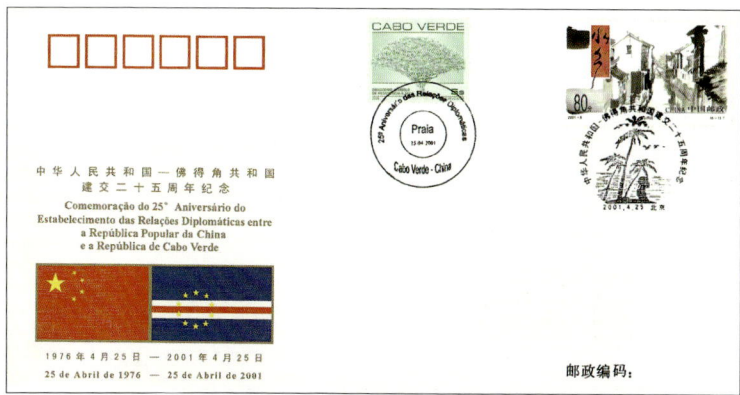

贴票：2001-5《水乡古镇》5 种随机贴用。佛得角邮票 1 种。
信封规格：208mm×110mm
纪念封、戳设计：马小玲
发行量：50 000 枚

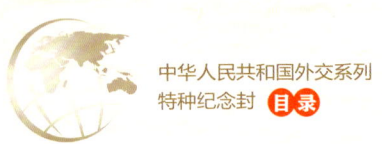

PFTN·WJ-64
中华人民共和国与圣马力诺共和国建交三十周年纪念封
The 30th Anniversary of the Establishment of Diplomatic Relations between the People's Republic of China and the Republic of San Marino — Commemorative Cover
2001 年 5 月 6 日发行

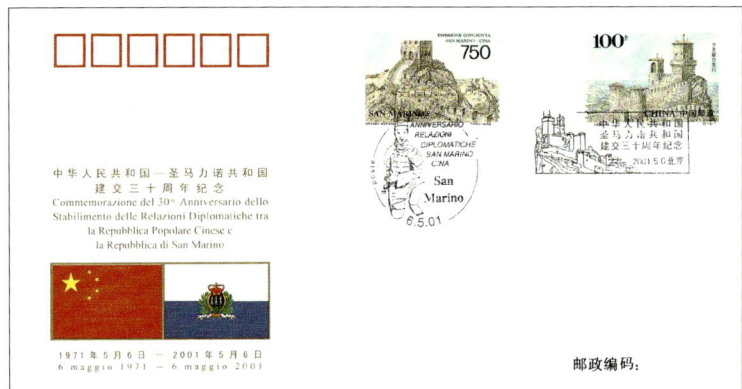

贴票：1996-8《古代建筑》1 种。圣马力诺邮票 5 种随机贴用。
信封规格：208mm×110mm
纪念封、戳设计：马小玲
发行量：50 000 枚

PFTN·WJ-65
中华人民共和国与巴基斯坦伊斯兰共和国建交五十周年纪念封
The 50th Anniversary of the Establishment of Diplomatic Relations between the People's Republic of China and the Islamic Republic of Pakistan — Commemorative Cover
2001 年 5 月 21 日发行

贴票：1999-11《中华人民共和国成立 50 周年—民族大团结》56 种、巴基斯坦邮票 4 种随机贴用。
信封规格：208mm×110mm
纪念封、戳设计：马小玲
发行量：50 000 枚

PFTN·WJ-66
中华人民共和国与奥地利共和国建交三十周年纪念封
The 30th Anniversary of the Establishment of Diplomatic Relations between the People's Republic of China and the Republic of Austria — Commemorative Cover
2001 年 5 月 28 日发行

贴票：2001-7《中国古典文学名著—聊斋志异（第一组）》2 种、奥地利邮票 8 种随机贴用。
信封规格：208mm×110mm
纪念封、戳设计：马小玲
发行量：50 000 枚

PFTN·WJ-67
中华人民共和国与苏里南共和国建交二十五周年纪念封
The 25th Anniversary of the Establishment of Diplomatic Relations between the People's Republic of China and the Republic of Suriname — Commemorative Cover
2001 年 5 月 28 日发行

贴票：2011-8《武当山》2 种随机贴用。
信封规格：208mm×110mm
纪念封、戳设计：马小玲
发行量：50 000 枚

中华人民共和国外交系列
特种纪念封 目录

附：加贴苏里南邮票（多种随机贴用）纪念活动用封

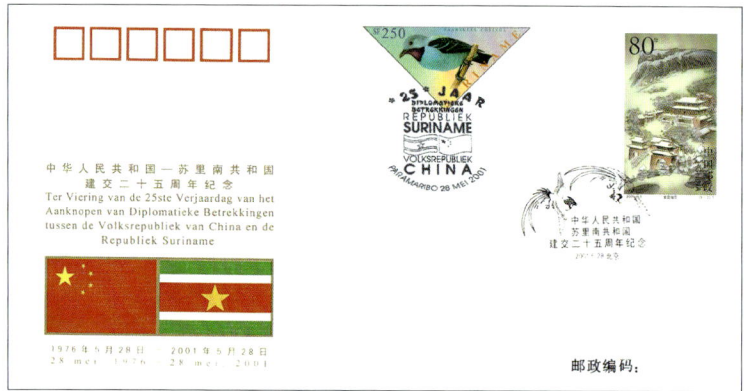

PFTN·WJ-68
中华人民共和国与阿拉伯埃及共和国建交四十五周年纪念封
The 45th Anniversary of the Establishment of Diplomatic Relations between the People's Republic of China and the Arab Republic of Egypt — Commemorative Cover
2001年5月30日发行

贴票：1997-23《长江三峡工程·截流》2枚
信封规格：208mm×110mm
纪念封、戳设计：马小玲
发行量：50 000枚

PFTN·WJ-69
中华人民共和国与塞舌尔共和国建交二十五周年纪念封
The 25th Anniversary of the Establishment of Diplomatic Relations between the People's Republic of China and the Republic of Seychelles — Commemorative Cover
2001 年 6 月 30 日发行

贴票：2001-10《端午节》2 种随机贴用。塞舌尔邮票 1 种。
信封规格：208mm×110mm
纪念封、戳设计：马小玲
发行量：50 000 枚

PFTN·WJ-70
中华人民共和国与塞拉利昂共和国建交三十周年纪念封
The 30th Anniversary of the Establishment of Diplomatic Relations between the People's Republic of China and the Republic of Sierra Leone — Commemorative Cover
2001 年 7 月 29 日发行

贴票：2000-25《中国古钟》1 种。塞拉利昂邮票多种随机贴用。
信封规格：208mm×110mm
纪念封、戳设计：马小玲
发行量：50 000 枚

PFTN·WJ-71
中华人民共和国与阿拉伯叙利亚共和国建交四十五周年纪念封
The 45th Anniversary of the Establishment of Diplomatic Relations between the People's Republic of China and the Syrian Arab Republic — Commemorative Cover
2001年8月1日发行

贴票：2001-13《黄果树瀑布》3种、叙利亚邮票5种随机贴用。
信封规格：208mm×110mm
纪念封、戳设计：马小玲
发行量：50 000枚
注：叙利亚邮戳国名S误为小写，后发行改正版。

PFTN·WJ-72
中华人民共和国与土耳其共和国建交三十周年纪念封
The 30th Anniversary of the Establishment of Diplomatic Relations between the People's Republic of China and the Republic of Turkey — Commemorative Cover
2001年8月4日发行

贴票：2000-21《中山靖王墓文物》1种
信封规格：208mm×110mm
纪念封、戳设计：马小玲
发行量：50 000枚

PFTN·WJ-73
中华人民共和国与伊朗伊斯兰共和国建交三十周年纪念封
The 30th Anniversary of the Establishment of Diplomatic Relations between the People's Republic of China and the Islamic Republic of Iran — Commemorative Cover
2001 年 8 月 16 日发行

贴票：1999-3《中国陶瓷—钧窑瓷器》1 种。伊朗邮票 6 种随机贴用。
信封规格：208mm×110mm
纪念封、戳设计：马小玲
发行量：50 000 枚

PFTN·WJ-74
中华人民共和国与爱沙尼亚共和国建交十周年纪念封
The 10th Anniversary of the Establishment of Diplomatic Relations between the People's Republic of China and the Republic of Estonia — Commemorative Cover
2001 年 9 月 11 日发行

贴票：2001-15《第 21 届世界大学生运动会》1 种。爱沙尼亚邮票 2 种随机贴用。
信封规格：208mm×110mm
纪念封、戳设计：马小玲
发行量：50 000 枚

PFTN·WJ-75
中华人民共和国与拉脱维亚共和国建交十周年纪念封
The 10th Anniversary of the Establishment of Diplomatic Relations between the People's Republic of China and the Republic of Latvia — Commemorative Cover
2001 年 9 月 12 日发行

贴票：1998-6《九寨沟》2 枚
信封规格：208mm×110mm
纪念封、戳设计：马小玲
发行量：50 000 枚

PFTN·WJ-76
中华人民共和国与立陶宛共和国建交十周年纪念封
The 10th Anniversary of the Establishment of Diplomatic Relations between the People's Republic of China and the Republic of Lithuania — Commemorative Cover
2001 年 9 月 14 日发行

贴票：2000-24《君子兰》2 种、立陶宛邮票 4 种随机贴用。
信封规格：208mm×110mm
纪念封、戳设计：马小玲
发行量：50 000 枚

PFTN·WJ-77
中华人民共和国与也门共和国建交四十五周年纪念封
The 45th Anniversary of the Establishment of Diplomatic Relations between the People's Republic of China and the Republic of Yemen — Commemorative Cover
2001 年 9 月 24 日发行

贴票：2001-14《北戴河》2 种、也门邮票 4 种随机贴用。
信封规格：208mm×110mm
纪念封、戳设计：马小玲
发行量：50 000 枚

PFTN·WJ-78
中华人民共和国与文莱达鲁萨兰国建交十周年纪念封
The 10th Anniversary of the Establishment of Diplomatic Relations between the People's Republic of China and Negara Brunei Darussalam — Commemorative Cover
2001 年 9 月 30 日发行

贴票：2001-18《兜兰》3 种、文莱邮票 4 种随机贴用。
信封规格：208mm×110mm
纪念封、戳设计：马小玲
发行量：50 000 枚

PFTN·WJ-79
中华人民共和国与巴布亚新几内亚独立国建交二十五周年纪念封
The 25th Anniversary of the Establishment of Diplomatic Relations between the People's Republic of China and the Independent State of Papua New Guinea — Commemorative Cover
2001 年 10 月 12 日发行

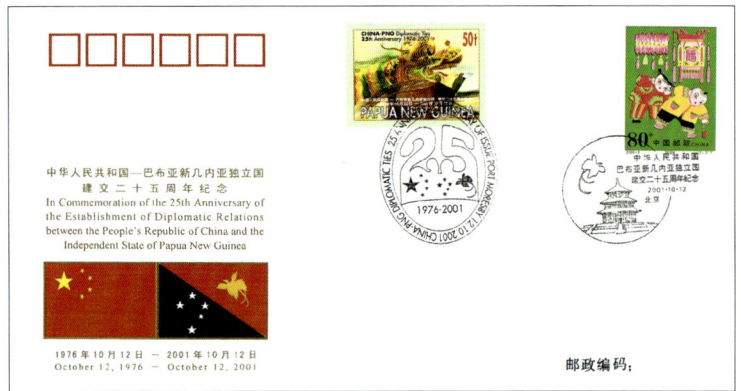

贴票：2000-2《春节》2 种、巴布亚新几内亚邮票 3 种随机贴用。
信封规格：208mm×110mm
纪念封、戳设计：马小玲
发行量：50 000 枚

PFTN·WJ-80
中华人民共和国与比利时王国建交三十周年纪念封
The 30th Anniversary of the Establishment of Diplomatic Relations between the People's Republic of China and the Kingdom of Belgium — Commemorative Cover
2001 年 10 月 25 日发行

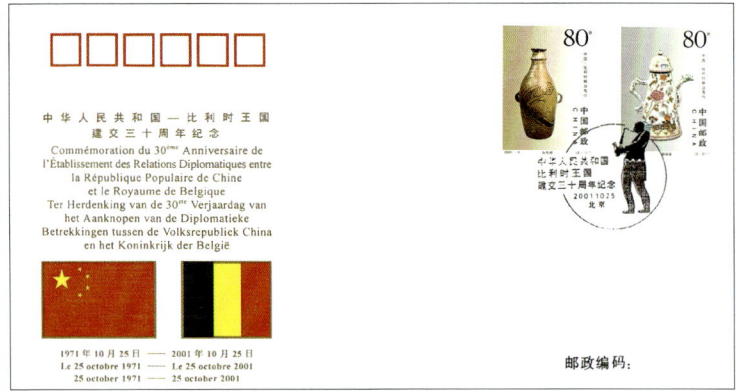

贴票：2001-9《陶瓷》2 枚
信封规格：208mm×110mm
纪念封、戳设计：马小玲
发行量：50 000 枚
注：信封背面比利时国名全称中的"王国"误为"共和国"，后发行改正版。

PFTN·WJ-81

中华人民共和国与秘鲁共和国建交三十周年纪念封
The 30th Anniversary of the Establishment of Diplomatic Relations between the People's Republic of China and the Republic of Peru — Commemorative Cover
2001 年 11 月 2 日发行

贴票：2001-21《亚太经合组织 2001 年会议·中国》1 枚
信封规格：208mm×110mm
纪念封、戳设计：马小玲
发行量：50 000 枚

附：加贴秘鲁邮票的纪念活动用封

PFTN·WJ-82
中华人民共和国与黎巴嫩共和国建交三十周年纪念封
The 30th Anniversary of the Establishment of Diplomatic Relations between the People's Republic of China and the Republic of Lebanon — Commemorative Cover
2001 年 11 月 9 日发行

贴票：2000-14《崂山》1 种。黎巴嫩邮票 1 种。
信封规格：208mm×110mm
纪念封、戳设计：马小玲
发行量：50 000 枚

PFTN·WJ-83
中华人民共和国与卢旺达共和国建交三十周年纪念封
The 30th Anniversary of the Establishment of Diplomatic Relations between the People's Republic of China and the Republic of Rwanda — Commemorative Cover
2001 年 11 月 12 日发行

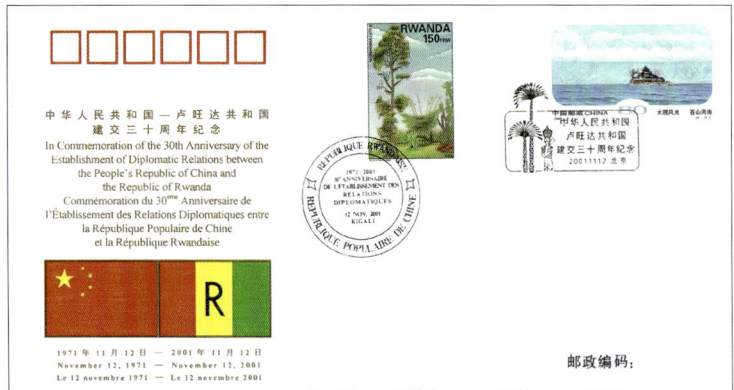

贴票：2000-8《大理风光》1 枚或 1995-18《联合国第四次世界妇女大会》2 枚。卢旺达邮票 8 种随机贴用。
信封规格：208mm×110mm
纪念封、戳设计：马小玲
发行量：50 000 枚

PFTN·WJ-84

中华人民共和国与冰岛共和国建交三十周年纪念封
The 30th Anniversary of the Establishment of Diplomatic Relations between the People's Republic of China and the Republic of Iceland — Commemorative Cover
2001 年 12 月 8 日发行

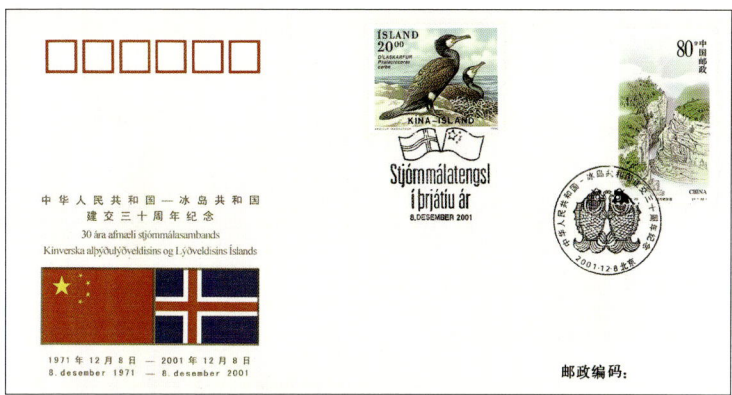

贴票：2001-25《六盘山》3 种、冰岛邮票 2 种随机贴用。
信封规格：208mm×110mm
纪念封、戳设计：马小玲
冰岛共和国纪念戳设计：赫里努尔·欧拉夫松
发行量：50 000 枚

PFTN·WJ-85

中华人民共和国与塞浦路斯共和国建交三十周年纪念封
The 30th Anniversary of the Establishment of Diplomatic Relations between the People's Republic of China and the Republic of Cyprus — Commemorative Cover
2001 年 12 月 14 日发行

贴票：2001-26《民间传说—许仙与白娘子》3 种随机贴用。塞浦路斯邮票 1 种。
信封规格：208mm×110mm
纪念封、戳设计：马小玲
发行量：50 000 枚

PFTN·WJ-86
中华人民共和国与乌兹别克斯坦共和国建交十周年纪念封
The 10th Anniversary of the Establishment of Diplomatic Relations between the People's Republic of China and the Republic of Uzbekistan — Commemorative Cover
2002 年 1 月 2 日发行

贴票：2001-18《兜兰》1 种。乌兹别克邮票 2 种随机贴用。
信封规格：208mm×110mm
纪念封、戳设计：马小玲
发行量：50 000 枚

PFTN·WJ-87
中华人民共和国与哈萨克斯坦共和国建交十周年纪念封
The 10th Anniversary of the Establishment of Diplomatic Relations between the People's Republic of China and the Republic of Kazakhstan — Commemorative Cover
2002 年 1 月 3 日发行

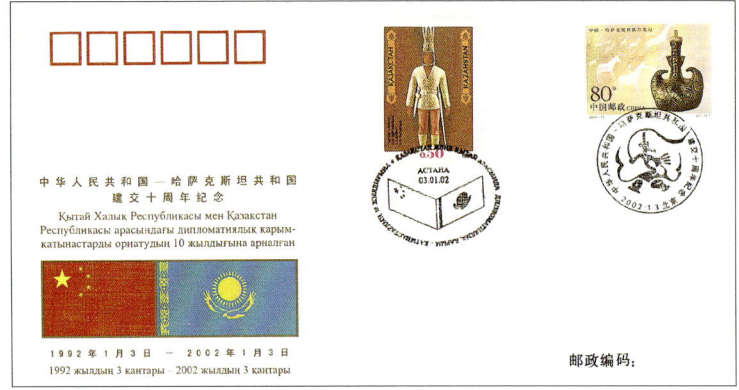

贴票：2000-13《盉壶和马奶壶》1 种。哈萨克斯坦邮票 2 种随机贴用。
信封规格：208mm×110mm
纪念封、戳设计：马小玲
发行量：50 000 枚

PFTN·WJ-88
中华人民共和国与乌克兰建交十周年纪念封
The 10th Anniversary of the Establishment of Diplomatic Relations between the People's Republic of China and Ukraine — Commemorative Cover
2002年1月4日发行

贴票：2000-23《气象成就》3种、乌克兰邮票6种随机贴用。
信封规格：208mm×110mm
纪念封、戳设计：马小玲
发行量：50 000枚
注：信封正面乌克兰国旗颜色不准确，后发行改正版。

PFTN·WJ-89
中华人民共和国与塔吉克斯坦共和国建交十周年纪念封
The 10th Anniversary of the Establishment of Diplomatic Relations between the People's Republic of China and the Republic of Tajikistan — Commemorative Cover
2002年1月4日发行

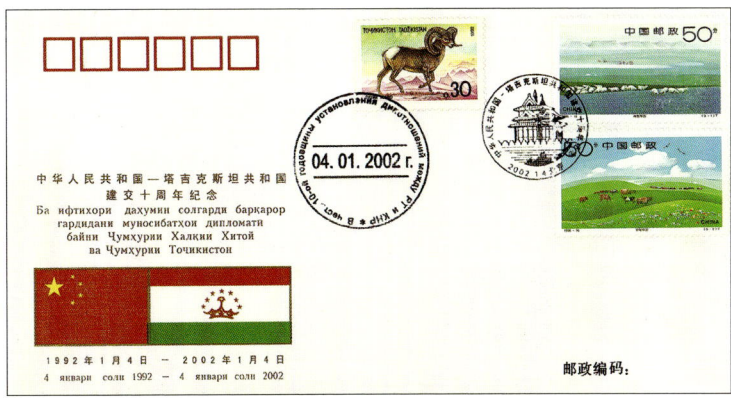

贴票：1998-16《锡林郭勒草原》2枚、塔吉克斯坦邮票1种。
信封规格：208mm×110mm
纪念封、戳设计：马小玲、胡·诺吉利
发行量：50 000枚

PFTN·WJ-90
中华人民共和国与吉尔吉斯共和国建交十周年纪念封
The 10th Anniversary of the Establishment of Diplomatic Relations between the People's Republic of China and the Kyrgyz Republic — Commemorative Cover
2002年1月5日发行

贴票：1996-19《天山天池》1枚或2枚拼贴。吉尔吉斯邮票7种随机贴用。
信封规格：208mm×110mm
纪念封、戳设计：马小玲
发行量：50 000 枚

PFTN·WJ-91
中华人民共和国与土库曼斯坦建交十周年纪念封
The 10th Anniversary of the Establishment of Diplomatic Relations between the People's Republic of China and Turkmenistan — Commemorative Cover
2002年1月6日发行

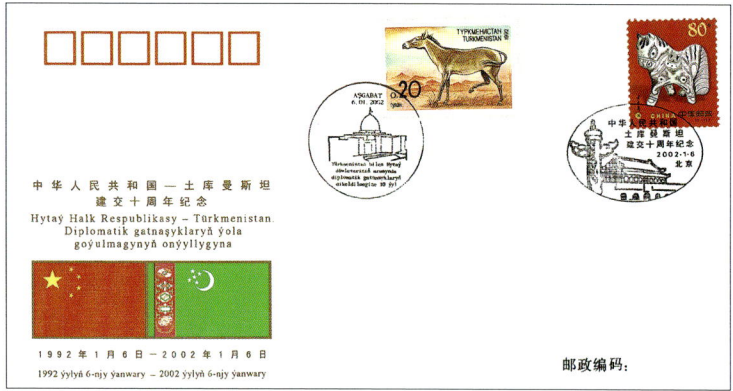

贴票：2002-1《壬午年》1种。土库曼斯坦邮票1种。
信封规格：208mm×110mm
纪念封、戳设计：马小玲
发行量：50 000 枚
注：信封背面外文说明将2002误为2001，后发行改正版。

PFTN·WJ-92
中华人民共和国与白俄罗斯共和国建交十周年纪念封
The 10th Anniversary of the Establishment of Diplomatic Relations between the People's Republic of China and the Republic of Belarus — Commemorative Cover
2002 年 1 月 20 日发行

贴票：2002-2《八大山人作品选》3 种、白俄罗斯邮票 2 种随机贴用。
信封规格：208mm×110mm
纪念封、戳设计：马小玲
发行量：50 000 枚

PFTN·WJ-93
中华人民共和国与以色列国建交十周年纪念封
The 10th Anniversary of the Establishment of Diplomatic Relations between the People's Republic of China and the State of Israel — Commemorative Cover
2002 年 1 月 24 日发行

贴票：2000-21《中山靖王墓文物》2 种、以色列邮票 3 种随机贴用。
信封规格：208mm×110mm
纪念封、戳设计：马小玲
发行量：50 000 枚

PFTN·WJ-94
中华人民共和国与摩尔多瓦共和国建交十周年纪念封
The 10th Anniversary of the Establishment of Diplomatic Relations between the People's Republic of China and the Republic of Moldova — Commemorative Cover
2002 年 1 月 30 日发行

贴票：2000-20《古代思想家》1 种。摩尔多瓦邮票多种随机贴用。
信封规格：208mm×110mm
纪念封、戳设计：马小玲
发行量：50 000 枚

PFTN·WJ-95
中华人民共和国与马耳他共和国建交三十周年纪念封
The 30th Anniversary of the Establishment of Diplomatic Relations between the People's Republic of China and the Republic of Malta — Commemorative Cover
2002 年 1 月 31 日发行

贴票：2000-24《君子兰》1 种。马耳他邮票 21 种随机贴用。
信封规格：208mm×110mm
纪念封、戳设计：马小玲
发行量：50 000 枚

PFTN·WJ-96（编号追加为 B1）
中华人民共和国驻阿富汗大使馆复馆纪念封
The People's Republic of China Embassy in Afghanistan museum complex Museum — Commemorative Cover
2002 年 2 月 6 日发行

贴票：普 31《中国鸟》1 元 1 枚
信封规格：208mm×110mm
纪念封、戳设计：马小玲、高峡
发行量：50 000 枚

附：加贴阿富汗邮票（多种随机贴用）纪念活动用封

53

PFTN·WJ-97
中华人民共和国与斯里兰卡民主社会主义共和国建交四十五周年纪念封
The 45th Anniversary of the Establishment of Diplomatic Relations between the People's Republic of China and the Democratic Socialist Republic of Sri Lanka — Commemorative Cover
2002年2月7日发行

贴票：2002-1《壬午年》1种。斯里兰卡邮票1种。
信封规格：208mm×110mm
纪念封、戳设计：马小玲
发行量：50 000 枚

PFTN·WJ-98
中华人民共和国与墨西哥合众国建交三十周年纪念封
The 30th Anniversary of the Establishment of Diplomatic Relations between the People's Republic of China and the United Mexican States — Commemorative Cover
2002年2月14日发行

贴票：普31《中国鸟》80分1枚。墨西哥邮票1种。
信封规格：208mm×110mm
纪念封、戳设计：马小玲
发行量：50 000 枚

PFTN·WJ-99
中华人民共和国与阿根廷共和国建交三十周年纪念封
The 30th Anniversary of the Establishment of Diplomatic Relations between the People's Republic of China and the Argentina Republic — Commemorative Cover
2002年2月19日发行

贴票：2000-4《龙（文物）》1种。阿根廷邮票4种随机贴用。
信封规格：208mm×110mm
纪念封、戳设计：马小玲
发行量：50 000枚
注：部分阿根廷纪念邮戳地名有误，后更正。

PFTN·WJ-100（编号追加为B2）
中美上海公报发表三十周年纪念封
The 30th Anniversary of the China-U.S. Shanghai Communique — Commemorative Cover
2002年2月28日发行

贴票：1994-15《鹤》2枚，或普31《中国鸟》2元1枚。
信封规格：208mm×110mm
纪念封、戳设计：马小玲
发行量：50 000枚

中华人民共和国外交系列
特种纪念封 目录

PFTN·WJ-101

中华人民共和国与大不列颠及北爱尔兰联合王国建立大使级外交关系三十周年纪念封
The 30th Anniversary of the Establishment of Diplomatic Relations at the Ambassadorial Level between the People's Republic of China and the United Kingdom of Great Britain and Northern Ireland — Commemorative Cover
2002 年 3 月 13 日发行

贴票：2002-4《民族乐器—拉弦乐器》3 种随机贴用。英国邮票 1 种。
信封规格：208mm×110mm
纪念封、戳设计：马小玲
发行量：50 000 枚

PFTN·WJ-102

中华人民共和国与瓦努阿图共和国建交二十周年纪念封
The 20th Anniversary of the Establishment of Diplomatic Relations between the People's Republic of China and the Republic of Vanuatu — Commemorative Cover
2002 年 3 月 26 日发行

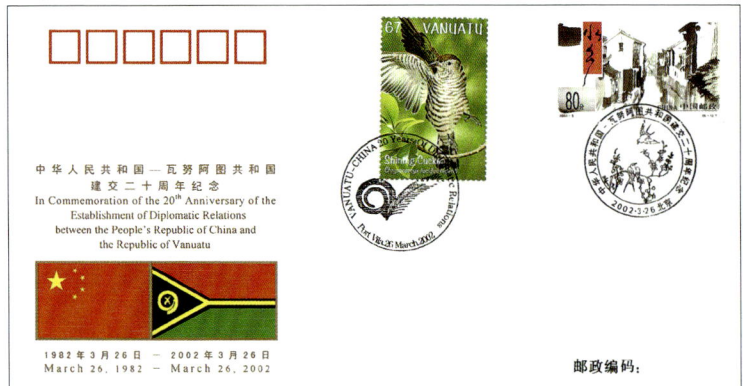

贴票：2001-5《水乡古镇》5 种随机贴用。瓦努阿图邮票 1 种。
信封规格：208mm×110mm
纪念封、戳设计：马小玲
发行量：50 000 枚

PFTN·WJ-103

中华人民共和国与阿塞拜疆共和国建交十周年纪念封
The 10th Anniversary of the Establishment of Diplomatic Relations between the People's Republic of China and the Republic of Azerbaijan — Commemorative Cover
2002 年 4 月 2 日发行

贴票：1999-11《中华人民共和国成立 50 周年—民族大团结》56 种随机贴用。阿塞拜疆邮票 1 种。
信封规格：208mm×110mm
纪念封、戳设计：马小玲
发行量：50 000 枚
注：部分纪念封只贴 1 枚阿塞拜疆邮票。

PFTN·WJ-104

中华人民共和国与亚美尼亚共和国建交十周年纪念封
The 10th Anniversary of the Establishment of Diplomatic Relations between the People's Republic of China and the Republic of Armenia — Commemorative Cover
2002 年 4 月 6 日发行

贴票：2002-6《中国陶瓷—汝窑瓷器》2 种、亚美尼亚邮票 16 种随机贴用。
信封规格：208mm×110mm
纪念封、戳设计：马小玲
发行量：50 000 枚

PFTN·WJ-105
中华人民共和国与约旦哈西姆王国建交二十五周年纪念封
The 25th Anniversary of the Establishment of Diplomatic Relations between the People's Republic of China and the Hashemite Kingdom of Jordan — Commemorative Cover
2002年4月7日发行

贴票：1997-16《黄山》8种、约旦邮票3种随机贴用。
信封规格：208mm×110mm
纪念封、戳设计：马小玲
发行量：50 000 枚

PFTN·WJ-106
中华人民共和国与毛里求斯共和国建交三十周年纪念封
The 30th Anniversary of the Establishment of Diplomatic Relations between the People's Republic of China and the Republic of Mauritius — Commemorative Cover
2002年4月15日发行

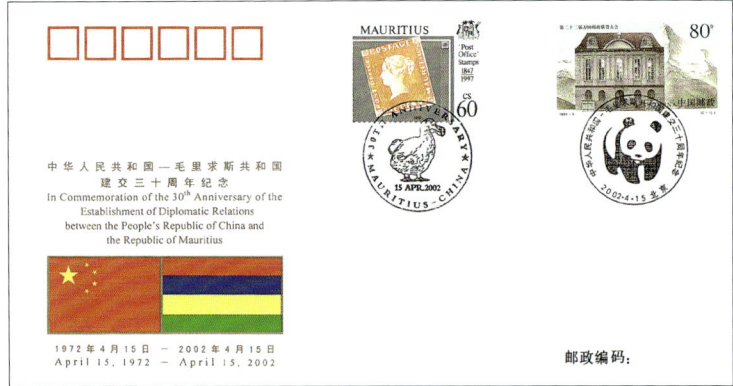

贴票：1999-9《第22届万国邮政联盟大会》1种。毛里求斯邮票1种。
信封规格：208mm×110mm
纪念封、戳设计：马小玲
发行量：50 000 枚

PFTN·WJ-107
中华人民共和国与斯洛文尼亚共和国建交十周年纪念封
The 10th Anniversary of the Establishment of Diplomatic Relations between the People's Republic of China and the Republic of Slovenia — Commemorative Cover
2002 年 5 月 12 日发行

贴票：2002-9《丽江古城》2 种、斯洛文尼亚邮票 2 种随机贴用。
信封规格：208mm×110mm
纪念封、戳设计：马小玲
发行量：50 000 枚

PFTN·WJ-108
中华人民共和国与克罗地亚共和国建交十周年纪念封
The 10th Anniversary of the Establishment of Diplomatic Relations between the People's Republic of China and the Republic of Croatia — Commemorative Cover
2002 年 5 月 13 日发行

贴票：普 30《保护人类共有的家园》80 分 1 枚。克罗地亚邮票 1 种。
信封规格：208mm×110mm
纪念封、戳设计：马小玲
发行量：50 000 枚

PFTN·WJ-109
中华人民共和国与巴巴多斯建交二十五周年纪念封
The 25th Anniversary of the Establishment of Diplomatic Relations between the People's Republic of China and Barbados — Commemorative Cover
2002年5月30日发行

贴票：2002-10《历史文物灯塔》5种、巴巴多斯邮票2种随机贴用。
信封规格：208mm×110mm
纪念封、戳设计：马小玲
发行量：50 000枚

PFTN·WJ-110
中华人民共和国与希腊共和国建交三十周年纪念封
The 30th Anniversary of the Establishment of Diplomatic Relations between the People's Republic of China and the Hellenic Republic — Commemorative Cover
2002年6月5日发行

贴票：个1《如意》专用邮票1枚。希腊邮票1种。
信封规格：208mm×110mm
纪念封、戳设计：马小玲
发行量：50 000枚

附：希腊邮政局、中国集邮总公司联合发行的《希腊共和国与中华人民共和国建交三十周年纪念封》

PFTN·WJ-111
中华人民共和国与格鲁吉亚建交十周年纪念封
The 10th Anniversary of the Establishment of Diplomatic Relations between the People's Republic of China and Georgia — Commemorative Cover
2002 年 6 月 9 日发行

贴票：2002-12《黄河水利水电工程》4 种、格鲁吉亚邮票 4 种随机贴用。
信封规格：208mm×110mm
纪念封、戳设计：马小玲
发行量：50 000 枚

PFTN·WJ-112
中华人民共和国与圭亚那合作共和国建交三十周年纪念封
The 30th Anniversary of the Establishment of Diplomatic Relations between the People's Republic of China and the Cooperative Republic of Guyana — Commemorative Cover
2002 年 6 月 27 日发行

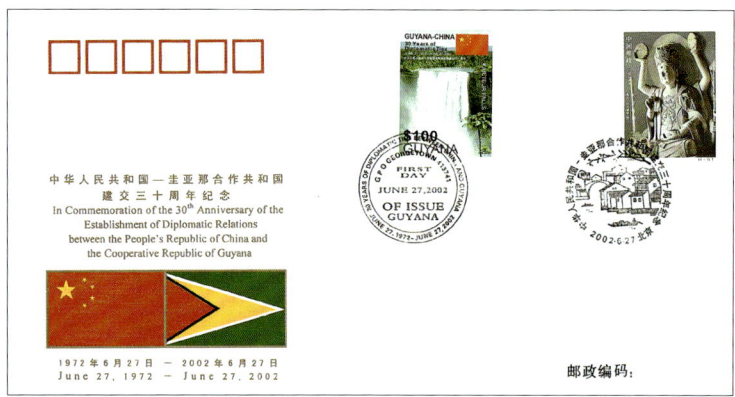

贴票：2002-13《大足石刻》4 种、圭亚那邮票 2 种随机贴用。
信封规格：208mm×110mm
纪念封、戳设计：马小玲
发行量：50 000 枚

PFTN·WJ-113
中华人民共和国与大韩民国建交十周年纪念封
The 10th Anniversary of the Establishment of Diplomatic Relations between the People's Republic of China and the Republic of Korea — Commemorative Cover
2002 年 8 月 24 日发行

贴票：2002-1《壬午年》1 种。韩国邮票 1 种。
信封规格：208mm×110mm
纪念封、戳设计：马小玲
发行量：50 000 枚

PFTN·WJ-114
中华人民共和国与多哥共和国建交三十周年纪念封
The 30th Anniversary of the Establishment of Diplomatic Relations between the People's Republic of China and the Republic of Togo — Commemorative Cover
2002 年 9 月 19 日发行

贴票：2002-16《青海湖》2 种、多哥邮票 4 种随机贴用。
信封规格：208mm×110mm
纪念封、戳设计：马小玲
发行量：50 000 枚

PFTN·WJ-115
中华人民共和国与日本国邦交正常化三十周年纪念封
The 30th Anniversary of the normalization of Diplomatic Relations between the People's Republic of China and Japan — Commemorative Cover
2002 年 9 月 29 日发行

贴票：2002-1《壬午年》1 种。日本邮票 3 种随机贴用。
信封规格：208mm×110mm
纪念封、戳设计：马小玲
发行量：50 000 枚

附：封内邮资明信片一枚

PFTN·WJ-116
中华人民共和国与德意志联邦共和国建交三十周年纪念封
The 30th Anniversary of the Establishment of Diplomatic Relations between the People's Republic of China and the Federal Republic of Germany — Commemorative Cover
2002年10月11日发行

贴票：1997-18《天坛》4种随机贴用2枚，或2002-13《大足石刻》4种随机贴用。
信封规格：208mm×110mm
纪念封、戳设计：马小玲
发行量：50 000枚
注：封面印有德国方面设计的纪念标志。

PFTN·WJ-117
中华人民共和国与马尔代夫共和国建交三十周年纪念封
The 30th Anniversary of the Establishment of Diplomatic Relations between the People's Republic of China and the Republic of Maldives — Commemorative Cover
2002年10月14日发行

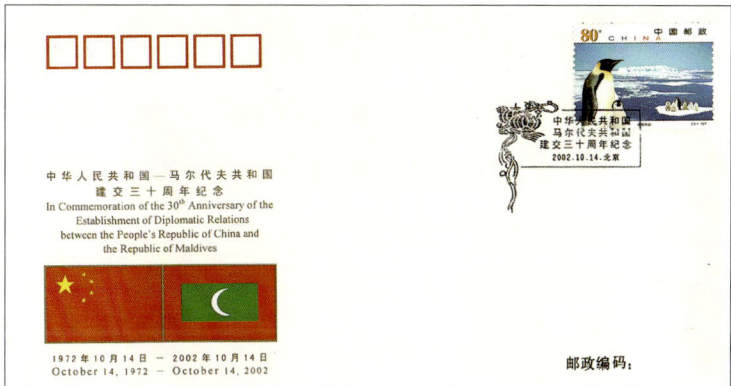

贴票：2002-15《南极风光》2种随机贴用
信封规格：208mm×110mm
纪念封、戳设计：马小玲
发行量：50 000枚

PFTN·WJ-118
中华人民共和国与乌干达共和国建交四十周年纪念封
The 40th Anniversary of the Establishment of Diplomatic Relations between the People's Republic of China and the Republic of Uganda — Commemorative Cover
2002年10月18日发行

贴票：2002-19《雁荡山》4种、乌干达邮票多种随机贴用。
信封规格：208mm×110mm
纪念封、戳设计：马小玲
发行量：50 000枚

PFTN·WJ-119
中华人民共和国与马达加斯加共和国建交三十周年纪念封
The 30th Anniversary of the Establishment of Diplomatic Relations between the People's Republic of China and the Republic of Madagascar — Commemorative Cover
2002年11月6日发行

贴票：2001-15《第21届世界大学生运动会》1种。马达加斯加邮票1种。
信封规格：208mm×110mm
纪念封、戳设计：马小玲
发行量：50 000枚

PFTN·WJ-120
中华人民共和国与卢森堡大公国建交三十周年纪念封
The 30th Anniversary of the Establishment of Diplomatic Relations between the People's Republic of China and the Grand Duchy of Luxembourg — Commemorative Cover
2002年11月16日发行

贴票：2002-25《博物馆建设》5种随机贴用
信封规格：208mm×110mm
纪念封、戳设计：马小玲
发行量：50 000枚

PFTN·WJ-121
中华人民共和国与牙买加建交三十周年纪念封
The 30th Anniversary of the Establishment of Diplomatic Relations between the People's Republic of China and Jamaica — Commemorative Cover
2002 年 11 月 21 日发行

贴票：2002-18《中国古代科学家（第四组）》4 种、牙买加邮票 2 种随机贴用。
信封规格：208mm×110mm
纪念封、戳设计：马小玲、马骁
发行量：50 000 枚

PFTN·WJ-122
中华人民共和国与澳大利亚联邦建交三十周年纪念封
The 30th Anniversary of the Establishment of Diplomatic Relations between the People's Republic of China and the Commonwealth of Australia — Commemorative Cover
2002 年 12 月 21 日发行

贴票：个 2《鲜花》专用邮票 1 枚。澳大利亚邮票 1 种。
信封规格：208mm×110mm
纪念封、戳设计：马小玲
发行量：50 000 枚

PFTN·WJ-123
中华人民共和国与新西兰建交三十周年纪念封
The 30th Anniversary of the Establishment of Diplomatic Relations between the People's Republic of China and New Zealand — Commemorative Cover
2002 年 12 月 22 日发行

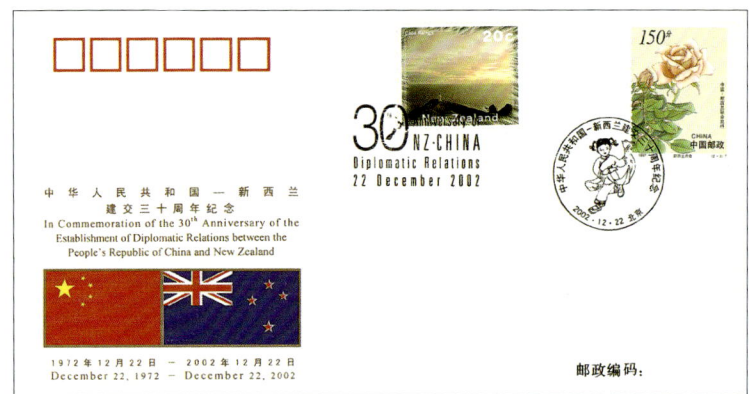

贴票：1997-17《花卉》1 枚或 2 枚，或个 1《如意》专用邮票 1 枚。新西兰邮票 2 种随机贴用。
信封规格：208mm×110mm
纪念封、戳设计：马小玲
发行量：50 000 枚

PFTN·WJ-124
中华人民共和国与贝宁共和国恢复外交关系三十周年纪念封
The 30th Anniversary of the restoration of Diplomatic Relations between the People's Republic of China and the Republic of Benin — Commemorative Cover
2002 年 12 月 29 日发行

贴票：个 1《如意》专用邮票 1 枚。贝宁邮票 6 种随机贴用。
信封规格：208mm×110mm
纪念封、戳设计：马小玲
发行量：50 000 枚

PFTN·WJ-125
中华人民共和国与安提瓜和巴布达建交二十周年纪念封
The 20th Anniversary of the Establishment of Diplomatic Relations between the People's Republic of China and Antigua and Barbuda — Commemorative Cover
2003年1月1日发行

贴票：2002-27《长臂猿》1种。安提瓜和巴布达邮票2种随机贴用。
信封规格：208mm×110mm
纪念封、戳设计：马小玲
发行量：50 000枚

PFTN·WJ-126
中华人民共和国与安哥拉共和国建交二十周年纪念封
The 20th Anniversary of the Establishment of Diplomatic Relations between the People's Republic of China and the Republic of Angola — Commemorative Cover
2003年1月12日发行

贴票：2003-1《癸未年》1种。安哥拉邮票4种随机贴用。
信封规格：208mm×110mm
纪念封、戳设计：马小玲
发行量：50 000枚

PFTN·WJ-127
中华人民共和国与乌拉圭东岸共和国建交十五周年纪念封
The 15th Anniversary of the Establishment of Diplomatic Relations between the People's Republic of China and the Oriental Republic of Uruguay — Commemorative Cover
2003年2月3日发行

贴票：2000-2《春节》3种、乌拉圭邮票2种随机贴用。
信封规格：208mm×110mm
纪念封、戳设计：马小玲
乌拉圭纪念戳设计：康斯坦丁诺·瓜索、莱昂纳多·瓜索
发行量：50 000枚
注：信封背面编号有误。后发行改正版。

PFTN·WJ-128
中华人民共和国与科特迪瓦共和国建交二十周年纪念封
The 20th Anniversary of the Establishment of Diplomatic Relations between the People's Republic of China and the Republic of Cote d'Ivoire — Commemorative Cover
2003年3月2日发行

贴票：2003-2《杨柳青木版年画》3种随机贴用。科特迪瓦邮票1种。
信封规格：208mm×110mm
纪念封、戳设计：马小玲
发行量：50 000枚
注：信封正面科特迪瓦共和国国旗颜色不准确，后发行改正版。

PFTN·WJ-129
中华人民共和国与西班牙建交三十周年纪念封
The 30th Anniversary of the Establishment of Diplomatic Relations between the People's Republic of China and Spain — Commemorative Cover
2003 年 3 月 9 日发行

贴票：2003-1《癸未年》1 种或 2003-4《百合花》3 种、西班牙邮票多种随机贴用。
信封规格：208mm×110mm
纪念封、戳设计：马小玲
发行量：50 000 枚

PFTN·WJ-130
中华人民共和国与厄立特里亚国建交十周年纪念封
The 10th Anniversary of the Establishment of Diplomatic Relations between the People's Republic of China and the State of Eritrea — Commemorative Cover
2003 年 5 月 24 日发行

贴票：2000-2《春节》2 种随机贴用。厄立特里亚邮票 1 种。
信封规格：208mm×110mm
纪念封、戳设计：马小玲
发行量：50 000 枚

PFTN·WJ-131
中华人民共和国与阿曼苏丹国建交二十五周年纪念封
The 25th Anniversary of the Establishment of Diplomatic Relations between the People's Republic of China and the Sultanate of Oman — Commemorative Cover
2003 年 5 月 25 日发行

贴票：1999-11《中华人民共和国成立 50 周年—民族大团结》56 种随机贴用。阿曼邮票 1 种。
信封规格：208mm×110mm
纪念封、戳设计：马小玲
发行量：50 000 枚

PFTN·WJ-132
中华人民共和国与卡塔尔国建交十五周年纪念封
The 15th Anniversary of the Establishment of Diplomatic Relations between the People's Republic of China and the State of Qatar — Commemorative Cover
2003 年 7 月 9 日发行

贴票：个 1《如意》或特 3-2001《中国加入世界贸易组织》1 枚。卡塔尔邮票 3 种随机贴用。
信封规格：208mm×110mm
纪念封、戳设计：马小玲
发行量：50 000 枚

PFTN·WJ-133
中华人民共和国与柬埔寨王国建交四十五周年纪念封
The 45th Anniversary of the Establishment of Diplomatic Relations between the People's Republic of China and the Kingdom of Cambodia — Commemorative Cover
2003 年 7 月 19 日发行

贴票：个 2《鲜花》1 枚。柬埔寨邮票 1 枚或 2 枚随机贴用，销票邮戳 2 种。
信封规格：208mm×110mm
纪念封、戳设计：马小玲、朱敏
发行量：50 000 枚

PFTN·WJ-134
中华人民共和国与大阿拉伯利比亚人民社会主义民众国建交二十五周年纪念封
The 25th Anniversary of the Establishment of Diplomatic Relations between the People's Republic of China and the Great Socialist People's Libyan Arab Jamahiriya— Commemorative Cover
2003 年 8 月 9 日发行

贴票：个 4《一帆风顺》专用邮票 1 枚。利比亚邮票多种随机贴用。
信封规格：208mm×110mm
纪念封、戳设计：马小玲
发行量：50 000 枚

PFTN·WJ-135（编号追加为 B3）
《中日和平友好条约》缔结二十五周年纪念封
The 25th Anniversary of the Establishment of "Sino Japanese Treaty of peace and friendship" — Commemorative Cover
2003 年 8 月 12 日发行

贴票：1997-16《黄山》8 种随机贴用
信封规格：208mm×110mm
纪念封、戳设计：马小玲、朱敏
发行量：50 000 枚

附：贴用 J104《中日青年友好联欢》1 种和日本邮票 1 种的纪念活动用封。

PFTN·WJ-136（编号追加为 B4）

德意志联邦共和国总统约翰内斯·劳对中华人民共和国进行国事访问纪念封
The State Visit to the People's Republic of China by H.E. Johannes Rau, President of the Federal Republic of Germany — Commemorative Cover
2003 年 9 月 10 日发行

贴票：1998-19《承德普宁寺和维尔茨堡宫》2 枚
信封规格：208mm×110mm
纪念封、戳设计：马小玲、朱敏
发行量：50 000 枚

PFTN·WJ-137

中华人民共和国与马其顿共和国建交十周年纪念封
The 10th Anniversary of the Establishment of Diplomatic Relations between the People's Republic of China and the Republic of Macedonia — Commemorative Cover
2003 年 10 月 12 日发行

贴票：个 5《天安门》加印中国国旗和马其顿国旗附票。马其顿邮票 4 种随机贴用。
信封规格：208mm×110mm
纪念封、戳设计：马小玲
发行量：50 000 枚

PFTN·WJ-138

中华人民共和国与摩洛哥王国建交四十五周年纪念封

The 45th Anniversary of the Establishment of Diplomatic Relations between the People's Republic of China and the Kingdom of Morocco — Commemorative Cover

2003 年 11 月 1 日发行

贴票：2003-20《民间传说—梁山伯与祝英台》4 种、摩洛哥邮票 2 种随机贴用。
信封规格：208mm×110mm
纪念封、戳设计：马小玲
发行量：50 000 枚

PFTN·WJ-139

中华人民共和国与汤加王国建交五周年纪念封

The 5th Anniversary of the Establishment of Diplomatic Relations between the People's Republic of China and the Kingdom of Tonga — Commemorative Cover

2003 年 11 月 2 日发行

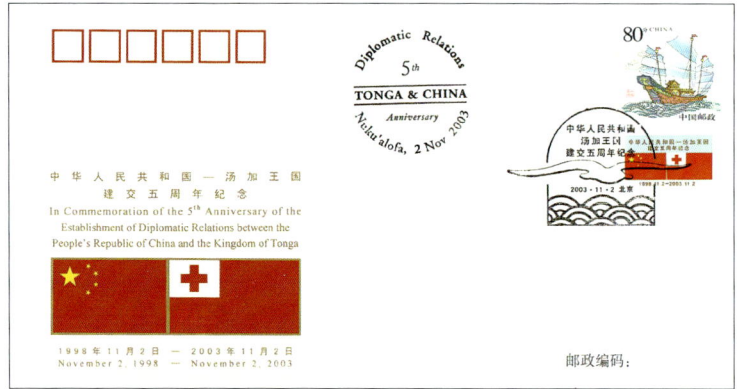

贴票：个 4《一帆风顺》加印中国国旗和汤加国旗附票
信封规格：208mm×110mm
纪念封、戳设计：马小玲
发行量：50 000 枚

附：加贴汤加邮票（2种随机贴用）纪念活动用封

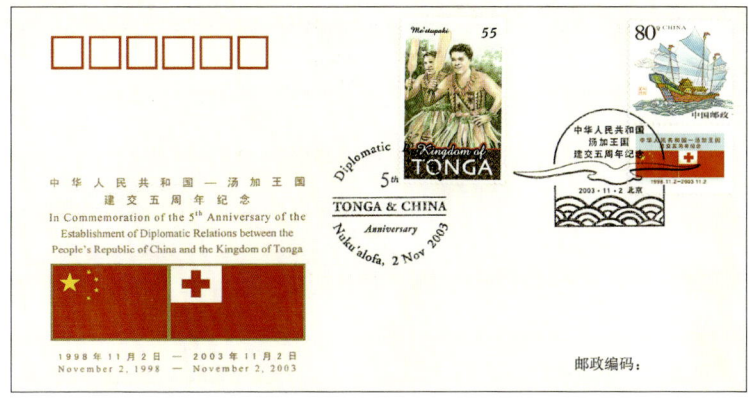

PFTN·WJ-140
中华人民共和国与肯尼亚共和国建交四十周年纪念封
The 40th Anniversary of the Establishment of Diplomatic Relations between the People's Republic of China and the Republic of Kenya — Commemorative Cover
2003年12月14日发行

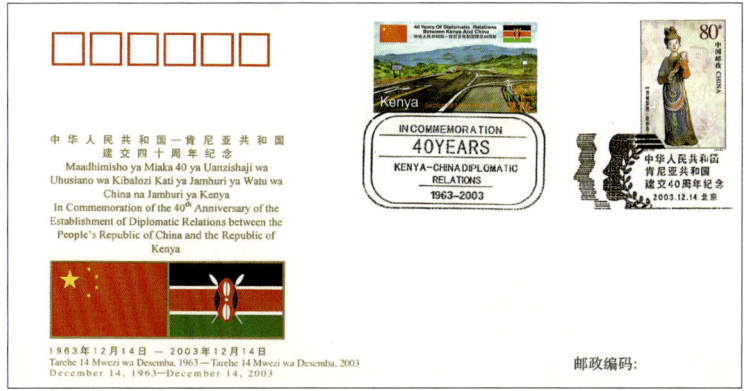

贴票：2003-15《晋祠彩塑》3种、肯尼亚邮票随机贴用1枚或2枚。
信封规格：208mm×110mm
纪念封、戳设计：马小玲
发行量：50 000枚

PFTN·WJ-141
中华人民共和国与阿尔及利亚民主人民共和国建交四十五周年纪念封
The 45th Anniversary of the Establishment of Diplomatic Relations between the People's Republic of China and the People's Democratic Republic of Algeria — Commemorative Cover
2003 年 12 月 20 日发行

贴票：2003-26《东周青铜器》4 种随机贴用。阿尔及利亚邮票 1 种。
信封规格：208mm×110mm
纪念封、戳设计：马小玲
发行量：50 000 枚

PFTN·WJ-142
中华人民共和国与吉布提共和国建交二十五周年纪念封
The 25th Anniversary of the Establishment of Diplomatic Relations between the People's Republic of China and the Republic of Djibouti — Commemorative Cover
2004 年 1 月 8 日发行

贴票：2003-5《中国古桥—拱桥》4 种、吉布提邮票 5 种随机贴用。
信封规格：208mm×110mm
纪念封、戳设计：马小玲
发行量：50 000 枚

PFTN·WJ-143
中华人民共和国与突尼斯共和国建交四十周年纪念封
The 40th Anniversary of the Establishment of Diplomatic Relations between the People's Republic of China and the Republic of Tunisia — Commemorative Cover
2004 年 1 月 10 日发行

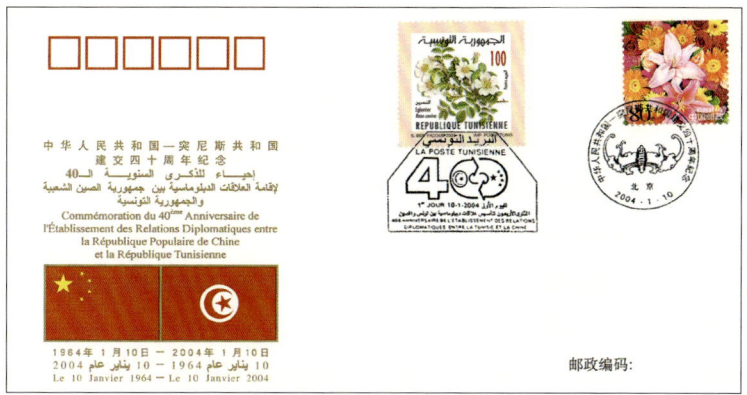

贴票：个 2《鲜花》1 枚。突尼斯邮票 1 种。
信封规格：208mm×110mm
纪念封、戳设计：马小玲
发行量：50 000 枚

PFTN·WJ-144
中华人民共和国与刚果共和国建交四十周年纪念封
The 40th Anniversary of the Establishment of Diplomatic Relations between the People's Republic of China and the Republic of Congo — Commemorative Cover
2004 年 2 月 22 日发行

贴票：2003-25《毛泽东同志诞生 110 周年》4 种、刚果邮票 3 种随机贴用。
信封规格：208mm×110mm
纪念封、戳设计：马小玲
发行量：50 000 枚

PFTN·WJ(B5)-145
中华人民共和国与加蓬共和国建交三十周年纪念封
The 30th Anniversary of the Establishment of Diplomatic Relations between the People's Republic of China and the Gabonese Republic — Commemorative Cover
2004 年 4 月 20 日发行

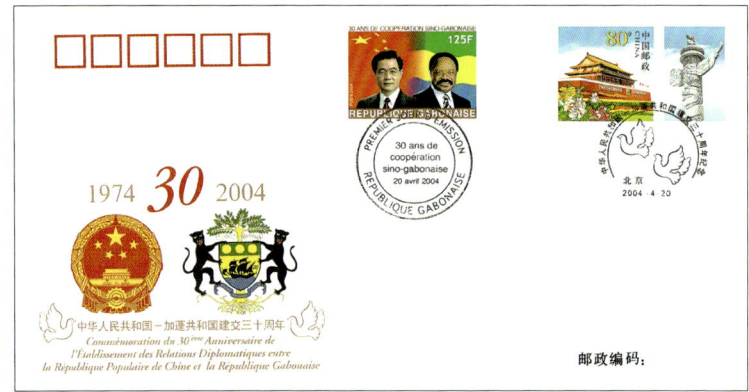

贴票：个 5《天安门》专用邮票 1 枚。加蓬邮票 2 种随机贴用。
信封规格：208mm×110mm
纪念封、戳设计：马小玲
发行量：50 000 枚

PFTN·WJ(B6)-146
和平解决朝鲜问题与恢复印度支那和平问题的日内瓦会议五十周年纪念封
The 50th Anniversary of the Geneva Conference on the Peaceful Settlement of the Korean Question and the Restoration of Peace in Indo-China — Commemorative Cover
2004 年 4 月 26 日发行

贴票：2004-6《孔雀》1 种
信封规格：208 mm×110mm
纪念封、戳设计：马小玲、黎家松
发行量：50 000 枚

PFTN·WJ(B7)-147

中华人民共和国与马来西亚建交三十周年暨中马友好年纪念封
The 30th Anniversary of the Establishment of Diplomatic Relations between the People's Republic of China and Malaysia and the Year of Friendship between China and Malaysia — Commemorative Cover
2004 年 5 月 31 日发行

贴票：个 4《一帆风顺》加印中国国旗和马来西亚国旗附票。马来西亚邮票 4 种随机贴用 1 枚或 2 枚。
信封规格：208mm×110mm
纪念封、戳设计：马小玲
发行量：50 000 枚

PFTN·WJ-148

中华人民共和国与爱尔兰建交二十五周年纪念封
The 25th Anniversary of the Establishment of Diplomatic Relations between the People's Republic of China and Ireland — Commemorative Cover
2004 年 6 月 22 日发行

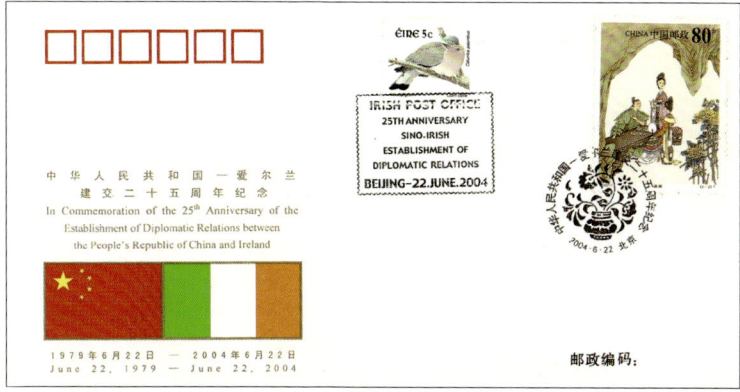

贴票：2002-7《中国古典文学名著—<聊斋志异>（第二组）》1 种。爱尔兰邮票 1 种。
信封规格：208mm×110mm
纪念封、戳设计：马小玲
发行量：50 000 枚

PFTN·WJ(B8)-149
和平共处五项原则创立五十周年纪念封
The 50th Anniversary of the Five Principles of Peaceful Coexistence — Commemorative Cover
2004 年 6 月 28 日、29 日发行
全套纪念封 2 枚

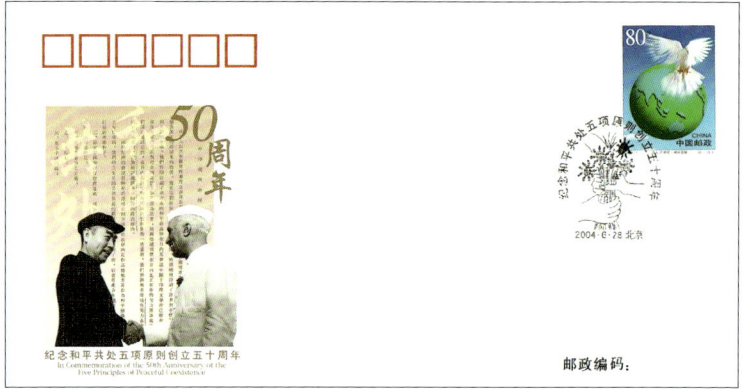

（2-1）

（2-2）

贴票：2001-1《世纪交替 千年更始—迈入 21 世纪》2 种随机贴用
信封规格：208 mm×110mm
纪念封、戳设计：马小玲、黎家松
发行量：50 000（套）

PFTN·WJ-150
中华人民共和国与安道尔公国建交十周年纪念封
The 10th Anniversary of the Establishment of Diplomatic Relations between the People's Republic of China and the Principality of Andorra — Commemorative Cover
2004 年 6 月 29 日发行

贴票：2004-5《成语典故（一）》1 种。安道尔邮票 4 种随机贴用。
信封规格：208mm×110mm
纪念封、戳设计：马小玲
发行量：50 000 枚

PFTN·WJ-151
中华人民共和国与密克罗尼西亚联邦建交十五周年纪念封
The 15th Anniversary of the Establishment of Diplomatic Relations between the People's Republic of China and the Federated States of Micronesia — Commemorative Cover
2004 年 9 月 11 日发行

贴票：2004-2《桃花坞木版年画》4 种，或 2004-17《邓小平同志诞生一百周年》2 种随机贴用。密克罗尼西亚邮票 6 种随机贴用。
信封规格：208mm×110mm
纪念封、戳设计：马小玲
发行量：50 000 枚

PFTN·WJ(B9)-152
法兰西共和国总统雅克·希拉克对中华人民共和国进行国事访问纪念封
The State Visit to the People's Republic of China by H.E. Jacques René Chirac, President of the Republic of France — Commemorative Cover
2004 年 10 月 8 日发行

贴票：1999-11《中华人民共和国成立 50 周年—民族大团结》56 种、法国邮票 2 种随机贴用。
信封规格：208mm×110mm
纪念封、戳设计：马小玲
发行量：50 000 枚

PFTN·WJ-153
中华人民共和国与阿富汗伊斯兰共和国建交五十周年纪念封
The 50th Anniversary of the Establishment of Diplomatic Relations between the People's Republic of China and the Islamic Republic of Afghanistan — Commemorative Cover
2005 年 1 月 20 日发行

贴票：2005-1《乙酉年》1 枚。阿富汗邮票 1 种。
信封规格：220mm×110mm
纪念封、戳设计：马小玲
发行量：50 000 枚

PFTN·WJ-154

中华人民共和国与波斯尼亚和黑塞哥维那建交十周年纪念封
The 10th Anniversary of the Establishment of Diplomatic Relations between the People's Republic of China and Bosnia and Herzegovina — Commemorative Cover
2005 年 4 月 3 日发行

贴票：个 8《长城》专用邮票 1 枚。波黑邮票 5 种随机贴用。
信封规格：220mm×110mm
纪念封、戳设计：马小玲
发行量：50 000 枚

PFTN·WJ(B10)-155

万隆会议五十周年纪念封
The 50th Anniversary of the Bandung Conference — Commemorative Cover
2005 年 4 月 18 日发行

贴票：1998-5《周恩来同志诞生 100 周年》4 种搭配贴用 2 枚
信封规格：220mm×110mm
纪念封、戳设计：马小玲
发行量：50 000 枚

PFTN·WJ-156

中华人民共和国与欧洲联盟建交三十周年纪念封
The 30th Anniversary of the Establishment of Diplomatic Relations between the People's Republic of China and the European Union — Commemorative Cover
2005年5月6日发行

贴票：个8《长城》加印"中欧建交30周年"附票
信封规格：220mm×110mm
纪念封、戳设计：马小玲
发行量：50 000 枚

PFTN·WJ(B11)-157

中华人民共和国与孟加拉人民共和国建交三十周年暨中孟友好年纪念封
The 30th Anniversary of the Establishment of Diplomatic Relations between the People's Republic of China and the People's Republic of Bangladesh and the Year of Friendship between China and Bangladesh — Commemorative Cover
2005年10月4日发行

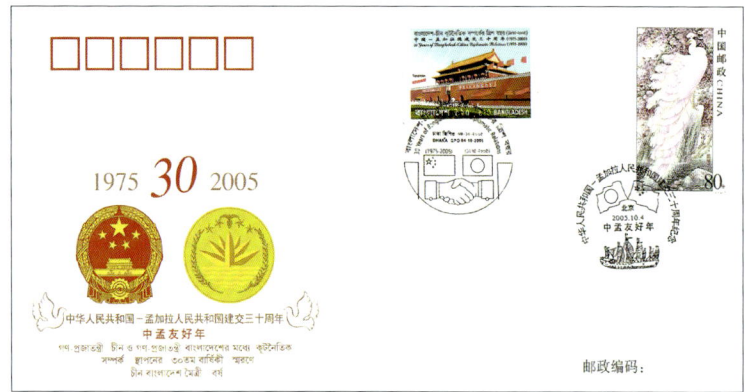

贴票：2004-6《孔雀》2种、孟加拉邮票4种随机贴用。
信封规格：220mm×110mm
纪念封、戳设计：马小玲
发行量：50 000 枚

PFTN·WJ-158
中华人民共和国与赤道几内亚共和国建交三十五周年纪念封
The 35th Anniversary of the Establishment of Diplomatic Relations between the People's Republic of China and the Republic of Equatorial Guinea — Commemorative Cover
2005年10月15日发行

贴票：2005-15《向海自然保护区》4种、赤道几内亚邮票5种随机贴用。
信封规格：220mm×110mm
纪念封、戳设计：马小玲
发行量：50 000 枚

PFTN·WJ-159
中华人民共和国与科摩罗联盟建交三十周年纪念封
The 30th Anniversary of the Establishment of Diplomatic Relations between the People's Republic of China and the Union of Comoros — Commemorative Cover
2005年11月13日发行

贴票：个9《五福临门》加印"花卉"附票100种随机贴用
信封规格：220mm×110mm
纪念封、戳设计：马小玲
发行量：50 000 枚

PFTN·WJ(B12)-160

巴基斯坦伊斯兰共和国总统佩尔韦兹·穆沙拉夫对中华人民共和国进行国事访问纪念封
The State Visit to the People's Republic of China by H.E.General Pervez Musharraf, President of the Islamic Republic of Pakistan — Commemorative Cover
2006年2月19日发行

贴票：2006-2《武强木版年画》4种、巴基斯坦邮票5种随机贴用。
信封规格：220mm×110mm
纪念封、戳设计：马小玲
发行量：50 000枚

PFTN·WJ(B13)-161

上海合作组织成立五周年纪念封
The 5th Anniversary of the Establishment of the Shanghai Cooperation Organization — Commemorative Cover
2006年6月15日发行

贴票：个9《五福临门》加印"上海合作组织成立五周年纪念"附票
信封规格：220mm×110mm
纪念封、戳设计：马小玲
发行量：50 000枚

附：加贴哈萨克斯坦、吉尔吉斯斯坦、俄罗斯、塔吉克斯坦、乌兹别克斯坦五国邮票的纪念活动用封

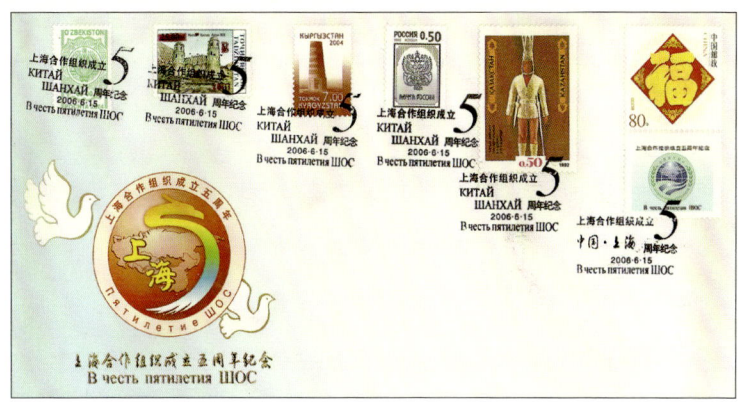

PFTN·WJ(B14)-162
中华人民共和国恢复在联合国合法席位三十五周年纪念封
The 35th Anniversary of the Restoration of the Lawful Rights of the People's Republic of China in the United Nations — Commemorative Cover
2006 年 10 月 25 日发行

贴票：2004-23《国旗国徽》"国旗"1 枚
信封规格：220 mm×110mm
纪念封、戳设计：马小玲
发行量：50 000 枚

PFTN·WJ(B15)-163
中非合作论坛北京峰会纪念封
The Beijing Summit of the Forum on China-Africa Cooperation — Commemorative Cover
2006 年 11 月 4 日发行

贴票：2006-20《中非合作论坛北京峰会》1 枚
信封规格：220mm×110mm
纪念封、戳设计：马小玲
发行量：50 000 枚

PFTN·WJ(B16)-164
塞浦路斯共和国总统帕帕佐普洛斯对中华人民共和国进行国事访问纪念封
The State Visit to the People's Republic of China by H.E. Tassos Papadopoulos, President of the Republic of Cyprus — Commemorative Cover
2006 年 12 月 4 日发行

贴票：普 30《中国鸟》1.20 元，或《中国鸟》40 分加 2005-28《第 29 届奥林匹克运动会——会徽和吉祥物》会徽 1 枚。
信封规格：220mm×110mm
纪念封、戳设计：马小玲
发行量：50 000 枚

PFTN·WJ(B17)-165
哈萨克斯坦共和国总统努·纳扎尔巴耶夫对中华人民共和国进行国事访问纪念封
The State Visit to the People's Republic of China by H.E. Nursultan Nazarbayev, President of the Republic of Kazakhstan — Commemorative Cover
2006 年 12 月 19 日发行

贴票：普 31《中国鸟》40 分加 1999-11《中华人民共和国成立 50 周年—民族大团结》56 种随机贴用
信封规格：220mm×110mm
纪念封、戳设计：马小玲
发行量：50 000 枚

PFTN·WJ-166
中华人民共和国与哥斯达黎加共和国建交纪念封
The Establishment of Diplomatic Relations between the People's Republic of China and the Republic of Costa Rica — Commemorative Cover
2007 年 6 月 1 日发行

贴票：2007-7《扬州园林》3 种随机贴用
信封规格：220mm×110mm
纪念封、戳设计：马小玲
发行量：50 000 枚

PFTN·WJ(B18)-167
西班牙国王胡安·卡洛斯一世对中华人民共和国进行国事访问纪念封
The State Visit to the People's Republic of China by H.E. Juan Carlos I, President of the Kingdom of Spain — Commemorative Cover
2007年6月24日发行

贴票：2004-25《城市建筑》2枚
信封规格：220mm×110mm
纪念封、戳设计：马小玲
发行量：50 000枚

PFTN·WJ(B19)-168
马其顿共和国总统布兰科·茨尔文科夫斯基对中华人民共和国进行国事访问纪念封
The State Visit to the People's Republic of China by H.E. Branko Crvenkovski, President of Macedonia — Commemorative Cover
2007年12月4日发行

贴票：特6-2007《中国探月首飞成功纪念》1枚
信封规格：220mm×110mm
纪念封、戳设计：马小玲
发行量：50 000枚
注：马其顿文信封名称和总统题词位置颠倒，后发行改正版。

附：加贴马其顿邮票的纪念活动用封

PFTN·WJ-169

中华人民共和国与南非共和国建交十周年纪念封
The 10th Anniversary of the Establishment of Diplomatic Relations between the People's Republic of China and the Republic of South Africa — Commemorative Cover
2008年1月1日发行

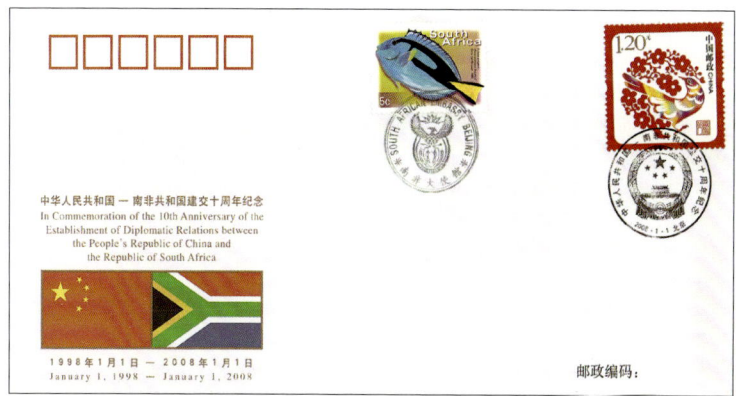

贴票：《喜上眉梢》1枚。南非邮票2种随机贴用。
信封规格：220mm×110mm
纪念封、戳设计：马小玲
发行量：50 000枚

PFTN·WJ(B20)-170

秘鲁共和国总统阿兰·加西亚·佩雷斯对中华人民共和国进行国事访问纪念封
The State Visit to the People's Republic of China by H.E. Alan Garcia Perez, President of the Republic of Peru — Commemorative Cover
2008 年 3 月 18 日发行

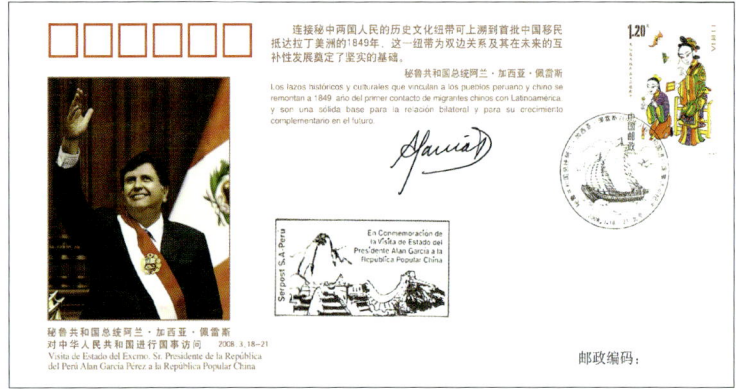

贴票：2008-2《朱仙镇木版年画》4 种随机贴用
信封规格：220mm×110mm
纪念封、戳设计：马小玲
发行量：50 000 枚

附：2005-28《第 29 届奥林匹克运动会 — 会徽和吉祥物》吉祥物 5 种随机贴用，并加贴秘鲁邮票（4 种随机贴用）纪念活动用封

94

PFTN·WJ(B21)-171

智利共和国总统米歇尔·巴切莱特·赫里亚对中华人民共和国进行国事访问纪念封
The State Visit to the People's Republic of China by H.E. Michelle Bachelet Jeria, President of the Republic of Chile — Commemorative Cover
2008年4月11日发行

贴票：《五福临门》2枚
信封规格：220mm×110mm
纪念封、戳设计：马小玲
发行量：50 000枚

附：加贴智利邮票的纪念活动用封

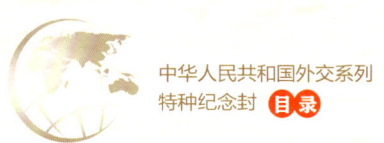

中华人民共和国外交系列
特种纪念封 目录

PFTN·WJ(B22)-172
汤加王国国王乔治·图普五世对中华人民共和国进行国事访问纪念封
The State Visit to the People's Republic of China by H.M. George Tupou V, King of the Kingdom of Tonga
— Commemorative Cover
2008年4月9日发行

贴票：《一帆风顺》2枚
信封规格：220mm×110mm
纪念封、戳设计：马小玲
发行量：50 000枚

附：加贴汤加邮票（4种随机贴用）纪念活动用封

PFTN·WJ(B23)-173

俄罗斯联邦总统德米特里·梅德韦杰夫对中华人民共和国进行国事访问纪念封
The State Visit to the People's Republic of China by H.E. Dmitry Anatolyevich Medvedev, President of the Russian Federation — Commemorative Cover
2008 年 5 月 23 日发行

贴票：个 5《天安门》2 枚，或个 1《如意》2 枚。
信封规格：220mm×110mm
纪念封、戳设计：马小玲
发行量：50 000 枚

附：加贴俄罗斯邮票（4 种随机贴用）纪念活动用封

中华人民共和国外交系列
特种纪念封 目录

PFTN·WJ(B24)-174

希腊共和国总统卡罗洛斯·帕普利亚斯对中华人民共和国进行国事访问纪念封
The State Visit to the People's Republic of China by H.E. Karolos Papoulias, President of the Hellenic Republic — Commemorative Cover
2008年6月23日发行

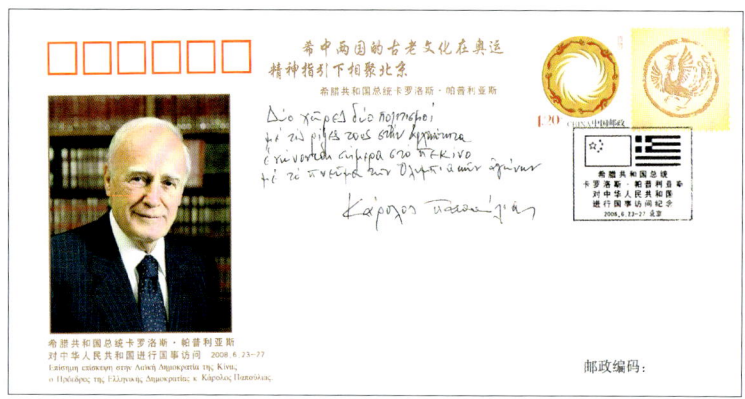

贴票：个13《太阳神鸟》专用邮票1枚
信封规格：220mm×110mm
纪念封、戳设计：马小玲
发行量：50 000枚

PFTN·WJ(B25)-175

联合国秘书长潘基文对中华人民共和国进行正式访问纪念封
The Official Visit to the People's Republic of China by H.E. Mr. Ban Ki-moon, Secretary of the United Nations — Commemorative Cover
2008年7月1日发行

贴票：特7-2008《抗震救灾 众志成城》附捐邮票1枚
信封规格：220mm×110mm
纪念封、戳设计：马小玲
发行量：50 000枚

附：加贴联合国邮票的纪念活动用封

PFTN·WJ-176
中华人民共和国与伊拉克共和国建交五十周年纪念封
The 50th Anniversary of the Establishment of Diplomatic Relations between the People's Republic of China and the Republic of Iraq — Commemorative Cover
2008 年 8 月 25 日发行

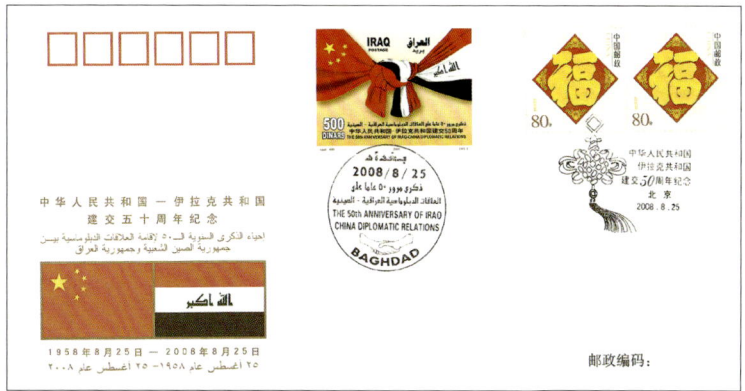

贴票：个9《五福临门》2枚。伊拉克邮票1种。
信封规格：220mm×110mm
纪念封、戳设计：马小玲
发行量：50 000 枚

PFTN·WJ-177
中华人民共和国与马来西亚建交三十五周年纪念封
The 35th Anniversary of the Establishment of Diplomatic Relations between the People's Republic of China and Malaysia — Commemorative Cover
2009年5月31日发行

贴票：2002-3《金花茶与炮弹花》2种、马来西亚邮票2种随机贴用。
信封规格：220mm×110mm
纪念封、戳设计：原艺珊
发行量：60 000枚

PFTN·WJ(B26)-178
塞尔维亚共和国总统鲍里斯·塔迪奇对中华人民共和国进行国事访问纪念封
The State Visit to the People's Republic of China by H.E. Boris Tadic, President of the Republic of Serbia — Commemorative Cover
2009年8月19日发行

贴票：个19《国旗》1枚。塞尔维亚邮票3种随机贴用。
信封规格：220mm×110mm
纪念封、戳设计：马小玲
发行量：50 000枚

PFTN·WJ-179
第二次中日韩领导人会议暨中日韩合作十周年纪念封
The Second Trilateral Summit Meeting among the People's Republic of China, Japan and the Republic of Korea, and the 10th Anniversary of trilateral among China, Japan and the Republic of Korea — Commemorative Cover
2009 年 10 月 10 日发行

贴票：2009-1《己丑年》1 枚
信封规格：220 mm×110mm
纪念封、戳设计：余晓亮
发行量：50 000 枚

2. 外交系列特种纪念封 C 系列

(PFTN·WJ(C)-1—PFTN·WJ(C)-29)

2006 年 5 月至 2009 年 9 月发行

PFTN·WJ(C)-1
中华人民共和国与阿拉伯埃及共和国建交五十周年纪念封
The 50th Anniversary of the Establishment of Diplomatic Relations between the People's Republic of China and the Arab Republic of Egypt — Commemorative Cover
2006 年 5 月 30 日发行

贴票：个 8《长城》加印"中埃友谊"附票。埃及邮票 2 种随机贴用。
信封规格：220mm×110mm
纪念封、戳设计：马小玲
发行量：50 000 枚
注：另有同图无编号纪念封，见 WH-10。

PFTN·WJ(C)-2
中华人民共和国与阿拉伯叙利亚共和国建交五十周年纪念封
The 50th Anniversary of the Establishment of Diplomatic Relations between the People's Republic of China and the Syrian Arab Republic — Commemorative Cover
2006 年 8 月 1 日发行

贴票：个 6《花开富贵》加印"中叙友谊"附票。叙利亚邮票 1 种。
信封规格：220mm×110mm
纪念封、戳设计：马小玲
发行量：50 000 枚

PFTN·WJ(C)-3
中华人民共和国与巴布亚新几内亚独立国建交三十周年纪念封
The 30th Anniversary of the Establishment of Diplomatic Relations between the People's Republic of China and the Independent State of Papua New Guinea — Commemorative Cover
2006 年 10 月 12 日发行

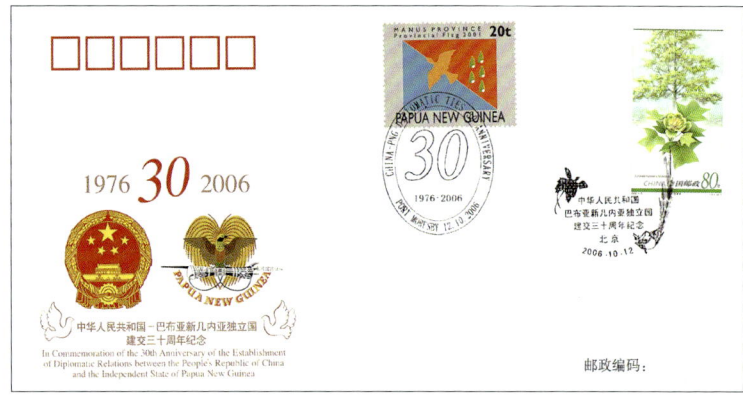

贴票：2006-5《孑遗植物》4 种、巴布亚新几内亚邮票 2 种随机贴用。
信封规格：220mm×10mm
纪念封、戳设计：马小玲
发行量：50 000 枚

PFTN·WJ(C)-4
中华人民共和国与秘鲁共和国建交三十五周年纪念封
The 35th Anniversary of the Establishment of Diplomatic Relations between the People's Republic of China and the Republic of Peru — Commemorative Cover
2006 年 11 月 2 日发行

贴票：2006-12《现代灯塔》4 种随机贴用
信封规格：220mm×110mm
纪念封、戳设计：马小玲
发行量：50 000 枚

附：加贴秘鲁邮票的纪念活动用封

PFTN·WJ(C)-5
中华人民共和国与乌兹别克斯坦共和国建交十五周年纪念封
The 15th Anniversary of the Establishment of Diplomatic Relations between the People's Republic of China and the Republic of Uzbekistan — Commemorative Cover
2007 年 1 月 2 日发行

贴票：普 31《中国鸟》40 分加 2006-23《文房四宝》4 种随机贴用。乌兹别克斯坦邮票 1 种。
信封规格：220mm×110mm
纪念封、戳设计：马小玲
发行量：50 000 枚

PFTN·WJ(C)-6
中华人民共和国与哈萨克斯坦共和国建交十五周年纪念封
The 15th Anniversary of the Establishment of Diplomatic Relations between the People's Republic of China and the Republic of Kazakhstan — Commemorative Cover
2007 年 1 月 3 日发行

贴票：2000-13《盉壶与马奶壶》2 枚
信封规格：220mm×110mm
纪念封、戳设计：马小玲
发行量：50 000 枚

PFTN·WJ(C)-7
中华人民共和国与乌克兰建交十五周年纪念封
The 15th Anniversary of the Establishment of Diplomatic Relations between the People's Republic of China and Ukraine — Commemorative Cover
2007 年 1 月 4 日发行

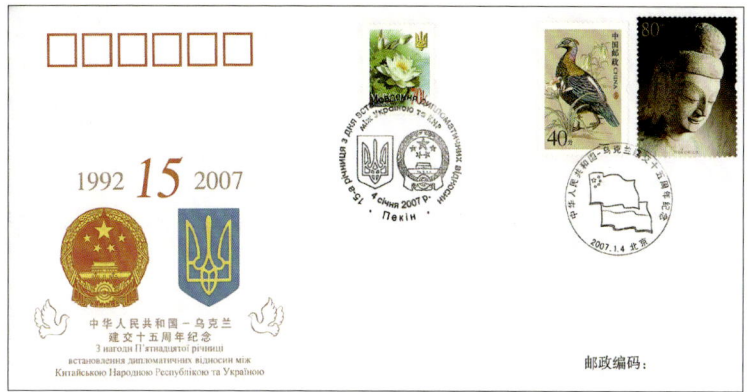

贴票：普 31《中国鸟》40 分加 2006-8《云冈石窟》4 种随机贴用。乌克兰邮票 2 种随机贴用。
信封规格：220mm×110mm
纪念封、戳设计：马小玲
发行量：50 000 枚

PFTN·WJ(C)-8
中华人民共和国与塔吉克斯坦共和国建交十五周年纪念封
The 15th Anniversary of the Establishment of Diplomatic Relations between the People's Republic of China and the Republic of Tajikistan — Commemorative Cover
2007 年 1 月 4 日发行

贴票：普 31《中国鸟》1.20 元 1 枚。塔吉克斯坦邮票 1 种。
信封规格：208mm×110mm
纪念封、戳设计：马小玲
发行量：50 000 枚

PFTN·WJ(C)-9
中华人民共和国与吉尔吉斯共和国建交十五周年纪念封
The 15th Anniversary of the Establishment of Diplomatic Relations between the People's Republic of China and the Kyrgyz Republic — Commemorative Cover
2007 年 1 月 5 日发行

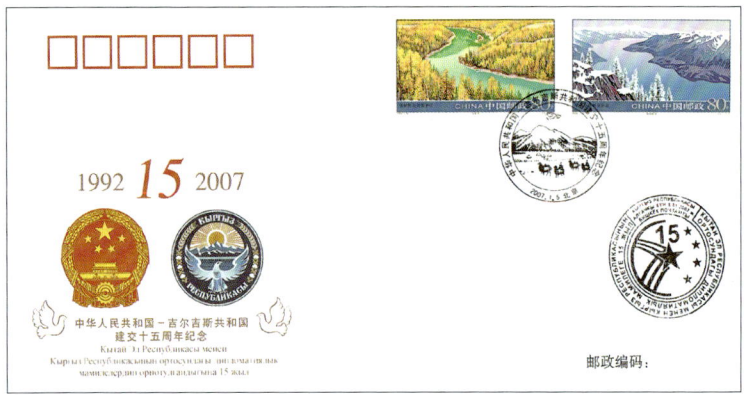

贴票：2006-16《喀纳斯自然保护区》4 种随机贴用 2 枚
信封规格：220mm×110mm
纪念封、戳设计：马小玲
发行量：50 000 枚

PFTN·WJ(C)-10
中华人民共和国与土库曼斯坦共和国建交十五周年纪念封
The 15th Anniversary of the Establishment of Diplomatic Relations between the People's Republic of China and Turkmenistan — Commemorative Cover
2007 年 1 月 6 日发行

贴票：2006-29《神骏图》2 种、土库曼斯坦邮票 2 种随机贴用。
信封规格：220mm×110mm
纪念封、戳设计：马小玲
发行量：50 000 枚

PFTN·WJ(C)-11

中华人民共和国与白俄罗斯共和国建交十五周年纪念封
The 15th Anniversary of the Establishment of Diplomatic Relations between the People's Republic of China and the Republic of Belarus — Commemorative Cover
2007年1月20日发行

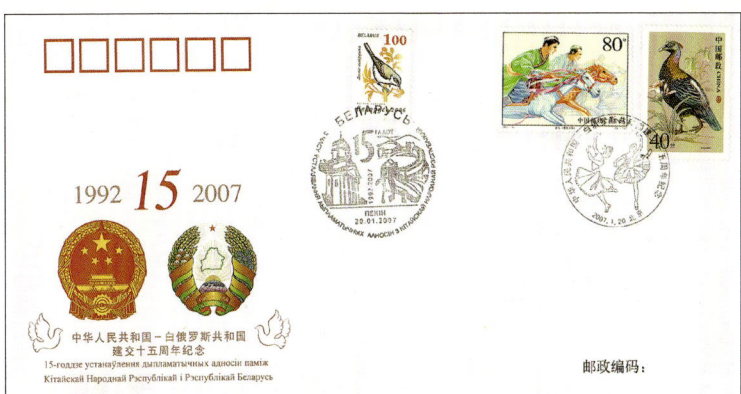

贴票：普31《中国鸟》40分加2003-16《少数民族传统体育》4种随机贴用。白俄罗斯邮票5种随机贴用。
信封规格：220mm×110mm
纪念封、戳设计：马小玲
发行量：50 000枚

PFTN·WJ(C)-12

中华人民共和国与摩尔多瓦共和国建交十五周年纪念封
The 15th Anniversary of the Establishment of Diplomatic Relations between the People's Republic of China and the Republic of Moldova — Commemorative Cover
2007年1月30日发行

贴票：个7《吉祥如意》加普31《中国鸟》40分。摩尔多瓦邮票多种随机贴用。
信封规格：220mm×110mm
纪念封、戳设计：马小玲
发行量：50 000枚

PFTN·WJ(C)-13

中华人民共和国与阿根廷共和国建交三十五周年纪念封
The 35th Anniversary of the Establishment of Diplomatic Relations between the People's Republic of China and the Argentina Republic — Commemorative Cover
2007 年 2 月 19 日发行

贴票：个 13《太阳神鸟》专用邮票。阿根廷邮票 2 种随机贴用。
信封规格：220mm×110mm
纪念封、戳设计：马小玲
发行量：50 000 枚

PFTN·WJ(C)-14

中华人民共和国与瓦努阿图共和国建交二十五周年纪念封
The 25th Anniversary of the Establishment of Diplomatic Relations between the People's Republic of China and the Republic of Vanuatu — Commemorative Cover
2007 年 3 月 26 日发行

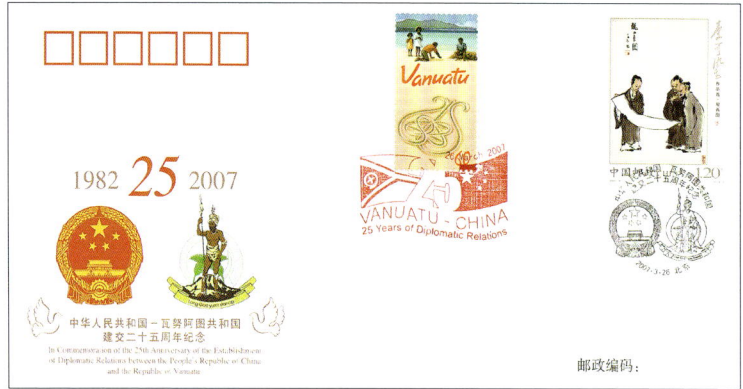

贴票：2007-6《李可染作品选》6 种随机贴用。瓦努阿图邮票 1 种。
信封规格：220mm×110mm
纪念封、戳设计：马小玲
发行量：50 000 枚

PFTN·WJ(C)

PFTN·WJ(C)-15
中华人民共和国与阿塞拜疆共和国建交十五周年纪念封
The 15th Anniversary of the Establishment of Diplomatic Relations between the People's Republic of China and the Republic of Azerbaijan — Commemorative Cover
2007年4月2日发行

贴票：个11《喜上眉梢》加普31《中国鸟》40分。阿塞拜疆邮票多种随机贴用。
信封规格：220mm×110mm
纪念封、戳设计：马小玲
发行量：50 000枚

PFTN·WJ(C)-16
中华人民共和国与亚美尼亚共和国建交十五周年纪念封
The 15th Anniversary of the Establishment of Diplomatic Relations between the People's Republic of China and the Republic of Armenia — Commemorative Cover
2004年4月6日发行

贴票：普31《中国鸟》40分加2004-27《中国名亭（一）》4种随机贴用。
信封规格：220mm×110mm
纪念封、戳设计：马小玲
发行量：50 000枚

111

PFTN·WJ(C)-17
中华人民共和国与斯洛文尼亚共和国建交十五周年纪念封
The 15th Anniversary of the Establishment of Diplomatic Relations between the People's Republic of China and the Republic of Slovenia — Commemorative Cover
2007 年 5 月 12 日发行

贴票：2006-29《神骏图》2 种、斯洛文尼亚邮票 4 种随机贴用。
信封规格：220mm×110mm
纪念封、戳设计：马小玲
发行量：50 000 枚

PFTN·WJ(C)-18
中华人民共和国与克罗地亚共和国建交十五周年纪念封
The 15th Anniversary of the Establishment of Diplomatic Relations between the People's Republic of China and the Republic of Croatia — Commemorative Cover
2007 年 5 月 13 日发行

贴票：2007-7《扬州园林》3 种、克罗地亚邮票 2 种随机贴用。
信封规格：220mm×110mm
纪念封、戳设计：马小玲
发行量：50000 枚

PFTN·WJ(C)-19

中华人民共和国与希腊共和国建交三十五周年纪念封
The 35th Anniversary of the Establishment of Diplomatic Relations between the People's Republic of China and the Hellenic Republic — Commemorative Cover
2007年6月5日发行

贴票：个14《第29届奥林匹克运动会火炬接力标志》专用邮票1枚
信封规格：208mm×110mm
纪念封、戳设计：马小玲
发行量：50 000枚

PFTN·WJ(C)-20

中华人民共和国与格鲁吉亚建交十五周年纪念封
The 15th Anniversary of the Establishment of Diplomatic Relations between the People's Republic of China and Georgia — Commemorative Cover
2007年6月9日发行

贴票：2007-14《孔融让梨》2种、格鲁吉亚邮票7种随机贴用。
信封规格：220mm×110mm
纪念封、戳设计：马小玲
发行量：50 000枚

PFTN·WJ(C)-21
中华人民共和国与新西兰建立外交关系三十五周年纪念封
The 35th Anniversary of the Establishment of Diplomatic Relations between the People's Republic of China and New Zealand — Commemorative Cover
2007 年 12 月 22 日发行

贴票：普 31《中国鸟》40 分加 2007-5《京剧生角》4 种随机贴用。新西兰邮票 1 种。
信封规格：220mm×110mm
纪念封、戳设计：马小玲
发行量：50 000 枚

PFTN·WJ(C)-22
中华人民共和国与乌拉圭东岸共和国建交二十周年纪念封
The 20th Anniversary of the Establishment of Diplomatic Relations between the People's Republic of China and the Oriental Republic of Uruguay — Commemorative Cover
2008 年 2 月 3 日发行

贴票：2008-1《戊子年》1 枚。乌拉圭邮票 2 种随机贴用。
信封规格：220mm×110mm
纪念封、戳设计：马小玲
发行量：50 000 枚

PFTN·WJ(C)

PFTN·WJ(C)-23
中华人民共和国与阿曼苏丹国建交三十周年纪念封
The 30th Anniversary of the Establishment of Diplomatic Relations between the People's Republic of China and the Sultanate of Oman — Commemorative Cover
2008年5月25日发行

贴票：2008-10《颐和园》6种随机贴用。阿曼邮票1种。
信封规格：220mm×110mm
纪念封、戳设计：马小玲
发行量：50 000枚

PFTN·WJ(C)-24
中华人民共和国与摩洛哥王国建交五十周年纪念封
The 50th Anniversary of the Establishment of Diplomatic Relations between the People's Republic of China and the Kingdom of Morocco — Commemorative Cover
2008年11月1日发行

贴票：个4《一帆风顺》2枚。摩洛哥邮票3种随机贴用。
信封规格：220mm×110mm
纪念封、戳设计：马小玲
发行量：50 000枚
注：部分纪念封贴用摩洛哥同图案丝绸邮票（3种随机贴用）。

115

PFTN·WJ(C)-25
中华人民共和国与阿尔及利亚民主人民共和国建交五十周年纪念封
The 50th Anniversary of the Establishment of Diplomatic Relations between the People's Republic of China and the People's Democratic Republic of Algeria — Commemorative Cover
2008年12月20日发行

贴票：2008-28《改革开放三十周年》1枚。阿尔及利亚邮票1种。
信封规格：220mm×110mm
纪念封、戳设计：马小玲
发行量：50 000枚

PFTN·WJ(C)-26
中华人民共和国与美利坚合众国建交三十周年纪念封
The 30th Anniversary of the Establishment of Diplomatic Relations between the People's Republic of China and the United States of America — Commemorative Cover
2009年1月1日发行

贴票：2009贺年专用邮票《花开富贵》1枚
信封规格：220mm×110mm
纪念封、戳设计：马小玲
发行量：50 000枚

PFTN·WJ(C)-27
中华人民共和国与苏丹共和国建交五十周年纪念封
The 50th Anniversary of the Establishment of Diplomatic Relations between the People's Republic of China and the Republic of Sudan — Commemorative Cover
2009 年 2 月 4 日发行

贴票：2009-1《己丑年》1 枚
信封规格：220mm×110mm
纪念封、戳设计：马小玲
发行量：50 000 枚

附：加贴苏丹邮票（3 种随机贴用）纪念活动用封

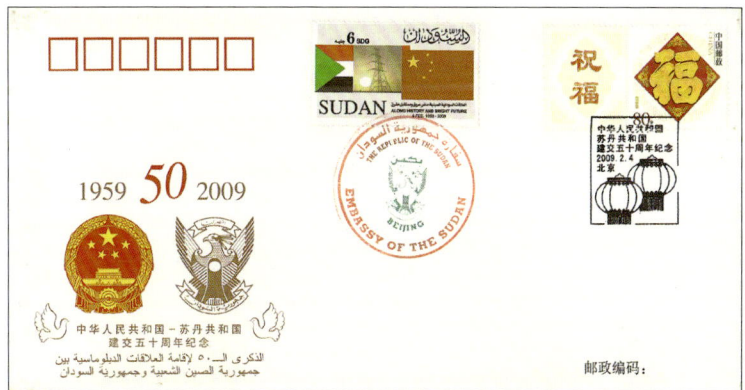

中华人民共和国外交系列 特种纪念封 目录

PFTN·WJ(C)-28
中华人民共和国与爱尔兰建交三十周年纪念封
The 30th Anniversary of the Establishment of Diplomatic Relations between the People's Republic of China and Ireland — Commemorative Cover
2009年6月22日发行

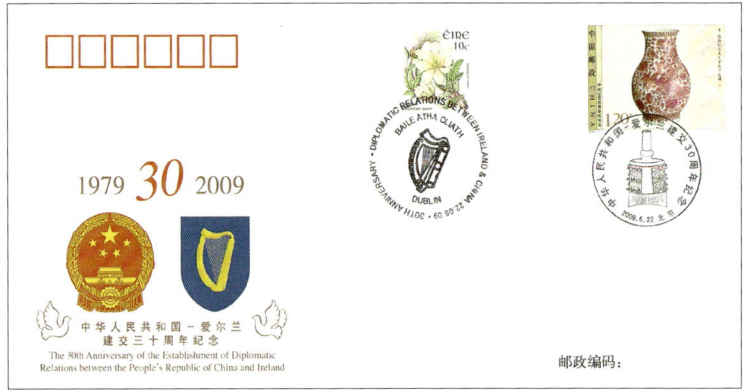

贴票：2009-7《中国2009世界集邮展览》2种随机贴用。爱尔兰邮票1种。
信封规格：220mm×110mm
纪念封、戳设计：马小玲
发行量：50 000枚

PFTN·WJ(C)-29
中华人民共和国与密克罗尼西亚联邦建交二十周年纪念封
The 20th Anniversary of the Establishment of Diplomatic Relations between the People's Republic of China and the Federated States of Micronesia — Commemorative Cover
2009年9月11日发行

贴票：2009-18《黄龙》3种、密克罗尼西亚邮票8种随机贴用。
信封规格：220mm×110mm
纪念封、戳设计：马小玲
发行量：50 000枚

3. 外交系列特种纪念封年度编号系列

（PFTN·WJ2010-1—PFTN·WJ2013-14）

2010年1月至2013年12月发行

PFTN·WJ2010-1
中华人民共和国与越南社会主义共和国建交六十周年纪念封
The 60th Anniversary of the Establishment of Diplomatic Relations between the People's Republic of China and the Socialist Republic of Viet Nam — Commemorative Cover
2010年1月18日发行

贴票：个17《和谐》加印中国国旗、越南国旗附票
信封规格：220mm×110mm
纪念封、戳设计：王墨雯
发行量：60 000枚

PFTN·WJ2010-2
中华人民共和国与格林纳达恢复外交关系五周年纪念封
The 5th Anniversary of the Resumption of Diplomatic Relations between the People's Republic of China and Grenada — Commemorative Cover
2010年1月20日发行

贴票：2010-1《庚寅年》1枚
信封规格：220mm×110mm
纪念封、戳设计：郭志义
发行量：60 000枚

PFTN·WJ2010-3
中华人民共和国与纳米比亚共和国建交二十周年纪念封
The 20th Anniversary of the Establishment of Diplomatic Relations between the People's Republic of China and the Republic of Namibia — Commemorative Cover
2010年3月22日发行

贴票：个17《和谐》加印中国国徽、纳米比亚国徽附票
信封规格：220mm×110mm
纪念封、戳设计：魏铮
发行量：60 000枚

PFTN·WJ2011

PFTN·WJ2011-1
巴西联邦共和国总统迪尔玛·罗塞芙对中华人民共和国进行国事访问纪念封
The State Visit to the People's Republic of China by H.E. Dilma Rousseff, President of the Federative Republic of Brazil — Commemorative Cover
2011 年 4 月 12 日发行

贴票：2011-1《辛卯年》1 枚
信封规格：220mm×110mm
纪念封、戳设计：马小玲
发行量：50 000 枚

PFTN·WJ2011-2
中华人民共和国与老挝人民民主共和国建交五十周年纪念封
The 50th Anniversary of the Establishment of Diplomatic Relations between the People's Republic of China and the Lao People's Democratic Republic — Commemorative Cover
2011 年 4 月 25 日发行

贴票：2008-2《朱仙镇木版年画》4 种随机贴用
信封规格：220mm×110mm
纪念封、戳设计：马小玲
发行量：50 000 枚

附：加贴老挝邮票的纪念活动用封

PFTN·WJ2011-3
中华人民共和国与圣马力诺共和国建交四十周年纪念封
The 40th Anniversary of the Establishment of Diplomatic Relations between the People's Republic of China and the Republic of San Marino — Commemorative Cover
2011 年 5 月 6 日发行

贴票：2010-3《上海世博园》1 种
信封规格：220mm×110mm
纪念封、戳设计：马小玲
发行量：50 000 枚

附：加贴圣马力诺邮票的纪念活动用封

PFTN·WJ2011-4
中华人民共和国与巴基斯坦伊斯兰共和国建交六十周年纪念封
The 60th Anniversary of the Establishment of Diplomatic Relations between the People's Republic of China and the Islamic Republic of Pakistan — Commemorative Cover
2011年5月21日发行

贴票：个17《和谐》专用邮票1枚
信封规格：220mm×110mm
纪念封、戳设计：马小玲
发行量：50 000枚

附：加贴巴基斯坦邮票（3种随机贴用）纪念活动用封

PFTN·WJ2011-5
中华人民共和国与奥地利共和国建交四十周年纪念封
The 40th Anniversary of the Establishment of Diplomatic Relations between the People's Republic of China and the Republic of Austria — Commemorative Cover
2011年5月28日

贴票：个17《和谐》专用邮票1枚
信封规格：220mm×110mm
纪念封、戳设计：马小玲
发行量：50 000枚

PFTN·WJ2011

附：加贴奥地利邮票的纪念活动用封

PFTN·WJ2011-6
中华人民共和国与苏里南共和国建交三十五周年纪念封
The 35th Anniversary of the Establishment of Diplomatic Relations between the People's Republic of China and the Republic of Suriname — Commemorative Cover
2011年5月28日发行

贴票：2010-3《上海世博园》1种
信封规格：220mm×110mm
纪念封、戳设计：马小玲
发行量：50 000枚

125

附：加贴苏里南邮票（4 种随机贴用）纪念活动用封

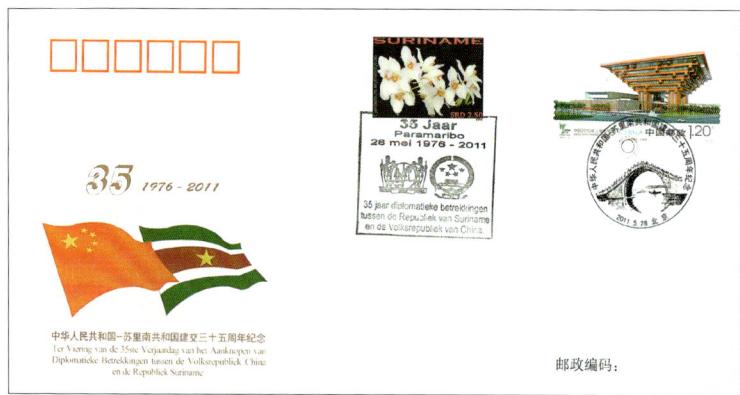

PFTN·WJ2011-7
中华人民共和国与黑山建交五周年纪念封
The 5th Anniversary of the Establishment of Diplomatic Relations between the People's Republic of China and Montenegro — Commemorative Cover
2011 年 7 月 6 日发行

贴票：个 20《音乐》专用邮票 1 枚
信封规格：220mm×110mm
纪念封、戳设计：马小玲
发行量：50 000 枚

PFTN·WJ2011

附：加贴黑山邮票（5 种随机贴用）纪念活动用封

PFTN·WJ2011-8
中华人民共和国与南苏丹共和国建交纪念封
The Establishment of Diplomatic Relations between the People's Republic of China and the Republic of South Sudan — Commemorative Cover
2011 年 7 月 9 日发行

贴票：个 19《国旗》专用邮票 1 枚
信封规格：220mm×110mm
纪念封、戳设计：马小玲
发行量：50 000 枚

附:加贴南苏丹邮票(3种随机贴用)纪念活动用封

PFTN·WJ2011-9
《中华人民共和国与俄罗斯联邦睦邻友好合作条约》签署十周年纪念封
The 10th Anniversary of signing of Treaty of Good-Neighborliness and Friendly Cooperation between the People's Republic of China and the Russian Federation — Commemorative Cover
2011年7月16日发行

贴票:个19《国旗》专用邮票1枚
信封规格:220mm×110mm
纪念封、戳设计:马小玲
发行量:50 000枚

附：加贴俄罗斯邮票（2种随机贴用）纪念活动用封

PFTN·WJ2011-10
中华人民共和国与东南亚国家联盟建立对话关系二十周年纪念封
The 20th Anniversary of the Establishment of Dialogue Relations between the People's Republic of China and Association of Southeast Asian Nations — Commemorative Cover
2011年7月19日发行

贴票：个20《音乐》专用邮票1枚
信封规格：220mm×110mm
纪念封、戳设计：马小玲
发行量：50 000枚

PFTN·WJ2011-11
喀麦隆共和国总统保罗·比亚对中华人民共和国进行国事访问纪念封
The State Visit to the People's Republic of China by H.E. Paul Biya, President of the Republic of Cameroon
— Commemorative Cover
2011 年 7 月 20 日发行

贴票：个 17《和谐》专用邮票 1 枚
信封规格：220mm×110mm
纪念封、戳设计：马小玲
发行量：50 000 枚

附：加贴喀麦隆邮票（4 种随机贴用）纪念活动用封

PFTN·WJ2011-12
中华人民共和国与塞拉利昂共和国建交四十周年纪念封
The 40th Anniversary of the Establishment of Diplomatic Relations between the People's Republic of China and the Republic of Sierra Leone — Commemorative Cover
2011年7月29日发行

贴票：个20《音乐》专用邮票1枚
信封规格：220mm×110mm
纪念封、戳设计：马小玲
发行量：50 000枚

附：加贴塞拉利昂邮票的纪念活动用封

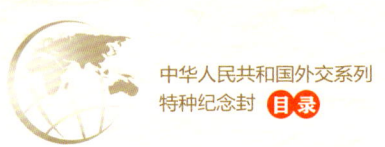

PFTN·WJ2011-13
中华人民共和国与爱沙尼亚共和国建交二十周年纪念封
The 20th Anniversary of the Establishment of Diplomatic Relations between the People's Republic of China and the Republic of Estonia — Commemorative Cover
2011年9月11日发行

贴票：2011-22《少数民族传统体育（二）》4种随机贴用
信封规格：220mm×110mm
纪念封、戳设计：马小玲
发行量：50 000 枚

附：加贴爱沙尼亚邮票的纪念活动用封

PFTN·WJ2011-14
中华人民共和国与拉脱维亚共和国建交二十周年纪念封
The 20th Anniversary of the Establishment of Diplomatic Relations between the People's Republic of China and the Republic of Latvia — Commemorative Cover
2011年9月12日发行

贴票：2011-18《曲艺》4种随机贴用
信封规格：220mm×110mm
纪念封、戳设计：马小玲
发行量：50 000枚

附：加贴拉脱维亚邮票（2种随机贴用）纪念活动用封

PFTN·WJ2011-15
中华人民共和国与立陶宛共和国建交二十周年纪念封
The 20th Anniversary of the Establishment of Diplomatic Relations between the People's Republic of China and the Republic of Lithuania — Commemorative Cover
2011年9月14日发行

贴票：2011-1《辛卯年》1枚
信封规格：220mm×110mm
纪念封、戳设计：马小玲
发行量：50 000枚

附：加贴立陶宛邮票的纪念活动用封

PFTN·WJ2011-16
中华人民共和国与文莱达鲁萨兰国建交二十周年暨中文友好年纪念封
The 20th Anniversary of the Establishment of Diplomatic Relations between the People's Republic of China and Negara Brunei Darussalam and the Year of Friendship between China and Brunei Darussalam — Commemorative Cover
2011 年 9 月 30 日发行

贴票：2009-8《中国与世博会》4 种随机贴用
信封规格：220mm×110mm
纪念封、戳设计：马小玲
发行量：50 000 枚

附：加贴文莱邮票（4 种随机贴用）纪念活动用封

PFTN·WJ2011-17
中华人民共和国与比利时王国建交四十周年纪念封
The 40th Anniversary of the Establishment of Diplomatic Relations between the People's Republic of China and the Kingdom of Belgium — Commemorative Cover
2011 年 10 月 25 日发行

贴票：个 23《花卉》专用邮票 10 种随机贴用
信封规格：220mm×110mm
纪念封、戳设计：马小玲
发行量：50 000 枚

PFTN·WJ2011-18
中华人民共和国与秘鲁共和国建交四十周年纪念封
The 40th Anniversary of the Establishment of Diplomatic Relations between the People's Republic of China and the Republic of Peru — Commemorative Cover
2011 年 11 月 2 日发行

贴票：2011-12《云锦》1 种
信封规格：220mm×110mm
纪念封、戳设计：马小玲
发行量：50 000 枚

附：加贴秘鲁邮票（8种随机贴用）纪念活动用封

PFTN·WJ2011-19
中华人民共和国与黎巴嫩共和国建交四十周年纪念封
The 40th Anniversary of the Establishment of Diplomatic Relations between the People's Republic of China and the Republic of Lebanon — Commemorative Cover
2011年11月9日发行

贴票：2009年贺年专用邮票《花开富贵》1枚
信封规格：208mm×110mm
纪念封、戳设计：马小玲
发行量：50 000枚

附：加贴黎巴嫩邮票（2种随机贴用）纪念活动用封

PFTN·WJ2011-20
中美"乒乓外交"四十周年纪念封
The 40th Anniversary of China-US Ping-Pong Diplomacy — Commemorative Cover
2011年11月发行

贴票：个23《花卉》专用邮票10种随机贴用
信封规格：220mm×110mm
纪念封、戳设计：马小玲
发行量：50 000枚

附：贴1994-15《鹤》邮票的纪念活动用封

PFTN·WJ2011-21
中华人民共和国与塞浦路斯共和国建交四十周年纪念封
The 40th Anniversary of the Establishment of Diplomatic Relations between the People's Republic of China and the Republic of Cyprus — Commemorative Cover
2011年12月14日发行

贴票：2012年贺年专用邮票《春和景明》1枚
信封规格：220mm×110mm
纪念封、戳设计：马小玲
发行量：50 000枚

附：加贴塞浦路斯邮票的纪念活动用封

PFTN·WJ2011-22
中国阿拉伯友好协会成立十周年纪念封
The 10th Anniversary of the Founding of the Chinese-Arab Friendship Association — Commemorative Cover
2011年12月21日发行

贴票：2010年贺年专用邮票《迎春纳福》1枚
信封规格：220mm×110mm
纪念封、戳设计：马小玲
发行量：50 000枚

PFTN·WJ2012-1
中华人民共和国与乌兹别克斯坦共和国建交二十周年纪念封
The 20th Anniversary of the Establishment of Diplomatic Relations between the People's Republic of China and the Republic of Uzbekistan — Commemorative Cover
2012 年 1 月 2 日发行

贴票：2009 年贺年专用邮票《花开富贵》1 枚
信封规格：220mm×110mm
纪念封、戳设计：马小玲
发行量：80 000 枚

PFTN·WJ2012-2
中华人民共和国与哈萨克斯坦共和国建交二十周年纪念封
The 20th Anniversary of the Establishment of Diplomatic Relations between the People's Republic of China and the Republic of Kazakhstan — Commemorative Cover
2012 年 1 月 3 日发行

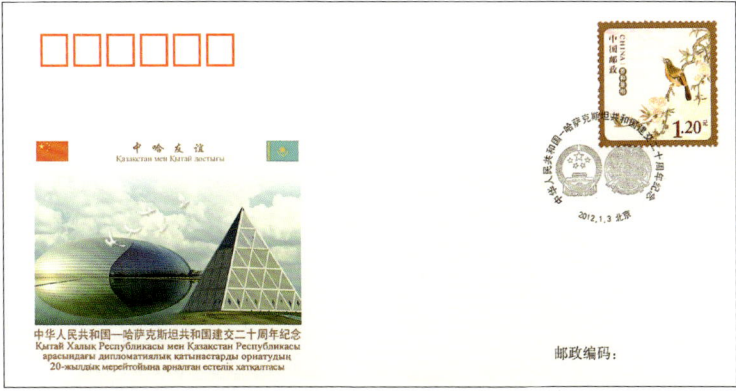

贴票：2012 年贺年专用邮票《春和景明》1 枚
信封规格：220mm×110mm
纪念封、戳设计：马小玲
发行量：80 000 枚

PFTN·WJ2012-3
中华人民共和国与乌克兰建交二十周年纪念封
The 20th Anniversary of the Establishment of Diplomatic Relations between the People's Republic of China and Ukraine — Commemorative Cover
2012年1月4日发行

贴票：2010年贺年专用邮票《迎春纳福》1枚
信封规格：220mm×110mm
纪念封、戳设计：马小玲
发行量：80 000枚

附：加贴乌克兰邮票（3种随机贴用）纪念活动用封

PFTN·WJ2012-4
中华人民共和国与塔吉克斯坦共和国建交二十周年纪念封
The 20th Anniversary of the Establishment of Diplomatic Relations between the People's Republic of China and the Republic of Tajikistan — Commemorative Cover
2012年1月4日发行

贴票：个20《音乐》专用邮票1枚
信封规格：220mm×110mm
纪念封、戳设计：马小玲
发行量：80 000枚

PFTN·WJ2012-5
中华人民共和国与吉尔吉斯共和国建交二十周年纪念封
The 20th Anniversary of the Establishment of Diplomatic Relations between the People's Republic of China and the Kyrgyz Republic — Commemorative Cover
2012年1月5日发行

贴票：2010年贺年专用邮票《迎春纳福》1枚
信封规格：220mm×110mm
纪念封、戳设计：马小玲
发行量：80 000枚

附：加贴吉尔吉斯邮票（4种随机贴用）纪念活动用封

PFTN·WJ2012-6
中华人民共和国与土库曼斯坦建交二十周年纪念封
The 20th Anniversary of the Establishment of Diplomatic Relations between the People's Republic of China and Turkmenistan — Commemorative Cover
2012年1月6日发行

贴票：2011-12《云锦》1种
信封规格：220mm×110mm
纪念封、戳设计：马小玲
发行量：80 000枚

附：加贴土库曼斯坦邮票（4种随机贴用）纪念活动用封

PFTN·WJ2012-7
中华人民共和国与白俄罗斯共和国建交二十周年纪念封
The 20th Anniversary of the Establishment of Diplomatic Relations between the People's Republic of China and the Republic of Belarus — Commemorative Cover
2012年1月20日发行

贴票：个20《音乐》专用邮票1枚。有加贴白俄罗斯邮票的纪念活动用封。
信封规格：220mm×110mm
纪念封、戳设计：马小玲
发行量：80 000枚

PFTN·WJ2012-8

中华人民共和国与以色列国建交二十周年纪念封
The 20th Anniversary of the Establishment of Diplomatic Relations between the People's Republic of China and the State of Israel — Commemorative Cover
2012年1月24日发行

贴票：个19《国旗》1枚
信封规格：220mm×110mm
纪念封、戳设计：马小玲
发行量：80 000枚

附：加贴以色列邮票的纪念活动用封

PFTN·WJ2012-9
中华人民共和国与摩尔多瓦共和国建交二十周年纪念封
The 20th Anniversary of the Establishment of Diplomatic Relations between the People's Republic of China and the Republic of Moldova — Commemorative Cover
2012年1月30日发行

贴票：个23《花卉》专用邮票10种随机贴用
信封规格：220mm×110mm
纪念封、戳设计：马小玲
发行量：80 000枚

附：加贴摩尔多瓦邮票（9种随机贴用）纪念活动用封

PFTN·WJ2012-10
中华人民共和国与马耳他共和国建交四十周年纪念封
The 40th Anniversary of the Establishment of Diplomatic Relations between the People's Republic of China and the Republic of Malta — Commemorative Cover
2012年1月31日发行

贴票：2009年贺年专用邮票《花开富贵》1枚
信封规格：220mm×110mm
纪念封、戳设计：马小玲
发行量：80 000枚

附：加贴马耳他邮票的纪念活动用封

148

PFTN·WJ2012-11
中华人民共和国与墨西哥合众国建交四十周年纪念封
The 40th Anniversary of the Establishment of Diplomatic Relations between the People's Republic of China and the United Mexican States — Commemorative Cover
2012 年 2 月 14 日发行

贴票：2012 年贺年专用邮票《春和景明》1 枚
信封规格：220mm×110mm
纪念封、戳设计：马小玲
发行量：80 000 枚

PFTN·WJ2012-12
中华人民共和国与阿根廷共和国建交四十周年纪念封
The 40th Anniversary of the Establishment of Diplomatic Relations between the People's Republic of China and the Argentina Republic — Commemorative Cover
2012 年 2 月 19 日发行

贴票：个 23《花卉》专用邮票 10 种随机贴用
信封规格：220mm×110mm
纪念封、戳设计：马小玲
发行量：80 000 枚

附：加贴阿根廷邮票的纪念活动用封

PFTN·WJ2012-13
中华人民共和国与大不列颠及北爱尔兰联合王国建立大使级外交关系四十周年纪念封
The 40th Anniversary of the Establishment of Diplomatic Relations at the Ambassadorial Level between the People's Republic of China and the United Kingdom of Great Britain and Northern Ireland — Commemorative Cover
2012年3月13日发行

贴票：2011-12《云锦》1枚
信封规格：220mm×110mm
纪念封、戳设计：马小玲
发行量：80 000 枚

PFTN·WJ2012-14
中华人民共和国与瓦努阿图共和国建交三十周年纪念封
The 30th Anniversary of the Establishment of Diplomatic Relations between the People's Republic of China and the Republic of Vanuatu — Commemorative Cover
2012 年 3 月 26 日发行

贴票：个 23《花卉》专用邮票 10 种随机贴用
信封规格：220mm×110mm
纪念封、戳设计：马小玲、邵吉平
发行量：80 000 枚

附：加贴瓦努阿图邮票的纪念活动用封（中国邮票或贴《花开富贵》贺年邮票 1 枚）

PFTN·WJ2012-15
中华人民共和国与阿塞拜疆共和国建交二十周年纪念封
The 20th Anniversary of the Establishment of Diplomatic Relations between the People's Republic of China and the Republic of Azerbaijan — Commemorative Cover
2012 年 4 月 2 日发行

贴票：个 23《花卉》专用邮票 10 种随机贴用
信封规格：220mm×110mm
纪念封、戳设计：马小玲
发行量：80 000 枚

附：加贴阿塞拜疆邮票（4 种随机贴用）纪念活动用封

PFTN·WJ2012-16
中华人民共和国与亚美尼亚共和国建交二十周年纪念封
The 20th Anniversary of the Establishment of Diplomatic Relations between the People's Republic of China and the Republic of Armenia — Commemorative Cover
2012 年 4 月 6 日发行

贴票：个 23《花卉》专用邮票 10 种随机贴用
信封规格：220mm×110mm
纪念封、戳设计：马小玲
发行量：80 000 枚

附：加贴亚美尼亚邮票（2 种随机贴用）纪念活动用封

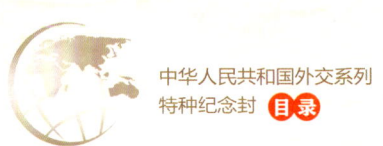

PFTN·WJ2012-17

中华人民共和国与毛里求斯共和国建交四十周年纪念封
The 40th Anniversary of the Establishment of Diplomatic Relations between the People's Republic of China and the Republic of Mauritius — Commemorative Cover
2012年4月15日发行

贴票：个23《花卉》专用邮票10种随机贴用
信封规格：220mm×110mm
纪念封、戳设计：马小玲
发行量：80 000枚

附：加贴毛里求斯邮票的纪念活动用封

PFTN·WJ2012-18
南苏丹共和国总统萨尔瓦·基尔·马亚尔迪特对中华人民共和国进行国事访问纪念封
The State Visit to the People's Republic of China by H.E. Gen.Salva Kiir Mayardit, President of the Republic of South Sudan — Commemorative Cover
2012 年 4 月 23 日发行

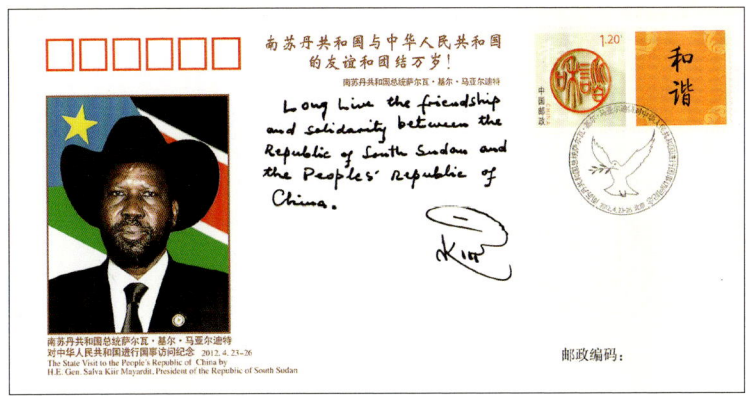

贴票：个 17《和谐》专用邮票 1 枚。有加贴南苏丹邮票（2 种随机贴用）纪念活动用封。
信封规格：220mm×110mm
纪念封、戳设计：马小玲
发行量：80 000 枚

PFTN·WJ2012-19
中华人民共和国与斯洛文尼亚共和国建交二十周年纪念封
The 20th Anniversary of the Establishment of Diplomatic Relations between the People's Republic of China and the Republic of Slovenia — Commemorative Cover
2012 年 5 月 12 日发行

贴票：2012-7《福禄寿喜》4 种随机贴用
信封规格：220mm110mm
纪念封、戳设计：马小玲
发行量：80 000 枚

附：加贴斯洛文尼亚邮票的纪念活动用封

PFTN·WJ2012-20
中华人民共和国与克罗地亚共和国建交二十周年纪念封
The 20th Anniversary of the Establishment of Diplomatic Relations between the People's Republic of China and the Republic of Croatia — Commemorative Cover
2012年5月13日发行

贴票：2012-7《福禄寿喜》4种随机贴用
信封规格：220mm×110mm
纪念封、戳设计：马小玲
发行量：80 000 枚

附：加贴克罗地亚邮票的纪念活动用封

PFTN·WJ2012-21
中华人民共和国与荷兰王国建立大使级外交关系四十周年纪念封
The 40th Anniversary of the Establishment of Diplomatic Relations at the Ambassadorial Level between the People's Republic of China and the Kingdom of the Netherlands — Commemorative Cover
2012 年 5 月 18 日发行

贴票：个 23《花卉》专用邮票 10 种随机贴用
信封规格：220mm×110mm
纪念封、戳设计：马小玲
发行量：80 000 枚
注：封面印有荷兰方面设计的纪念标志。纪念活动用此封，另加盖相关戳记。

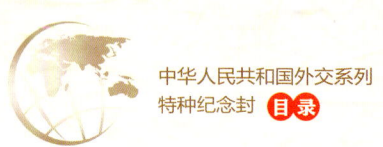

PFTN·WJ2012-22
中华人民共和国与东帝汶民主共和国建交十周年纪念封
The 10th Anniversary of the Establishment of Diplomatic Relations between the People's Republic of China and the Democratic Republic of Timor-Leste — Commemorative Cover
2012年5月20日发行

贴票：2010年贺年专用邮票《迎春纳福》1枚
信封规格：220mm×110mm
纪念封、戳设计：马小玲
发行量：80 000枚

附：加贴东帝汶邮票（4种随机贴用）纪念活动用封

PFTN·WJ2012-23
哥伦比亚共和国总统胡安·曼努埃尔·桑托斯·卡尔德龙对中华人民共和国进行国事访问纪念封
The State Visit to the People's Republic of China by H.E. Juan Manuel Santos Calderon, President of the Republic of Columbia — Commemorative Cover
2012 年 5 月 8 日发行

贴票：个 17《和谐》1 枚
信封规格：220mm×110mm
纪念封、戳设计：马小玲
发行量：80 000 枚

PFTN·WJ2012-24
中华人民共和国与巴哈马国建交十五周年纪念封
The 15th Anniversary of the Establishment of Diplomatic Relations between the People's Republic of China and the Commonwealth of the Bahamas — Commemorative Cover
2012 年 5 月 23 日发行

贴票：个 23《花卉》专用邮票 10 种随机贴用
信封规格：220mm×110mm
纪念封、戳设计：马小玲
发行量：80 000 枚

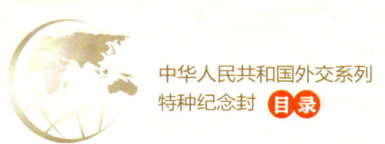

附：加贴巴哈马邮票的纪念活动用封

PFTN·WJ2012-25
中华人民共和国与巴巴多斯建交三十五周年纪念封
The 35th Anniversary of the Establishment of Diplomatic Relations between the People's Republic of China and Barbados — Commemorative Cover
2012年6月1日发行

贴票：个23《花卉》专用邮票10种随机贴用
信封规格：220mm×110mm
纪念封、戳设计：马小玲
发行量：80 000 枚

PFTN·WJ2012

附:加贴巴巴多斯邮票(6种随机贴用)纪念活动用封

PFTN·WJ2012-26
中华人民共和国与哥斯达黎加共和国建交五周年纪念封
The 5th Anniversary of the Establishment of Diplomatic Relations between the People's Republic of China and the Republic of Costa Rica — Commemorative Cover
2012年6月1日发行

贴票:个20《音乐》专用邮票1枚
信封规格:220mm×110mm
纪念封、戳设计:马小玲
发行量:80 000枚

PFTN·WJ2012-27
中华人民共和国与希腊共和国建交四十周年纪念封
The 40th Anniversary of the Establishment of Diplomatic Relations between the People's Republic of China and the Hellenic Republic — Commemorative Cover
2012年6月5日发行

贴票：个23《花卉》专用邮票10种随机贴用
信封规格：220mm×110mm
纪念封、戳设计：马小玲
发行量：80 000枚

附：加贴希腊邮票的纪念活动用封

PFTN·WJ2012-28
中华人民共和国与格鲁吉亚建交二十周年纪念封
The 20th Anniversary of the Establishment of Diplomatic Relations between the People's Republic of China and Georgia — Commemorative Cover
2012 年 6 月 9 日发行

贴票：个 23《花卉》专用邮票 10 种随机贴用
信封规格：220mm×110mm
纪念封、戳设计：马小玲
发行量：80 000 枚

PFTN·WJ2012-29
中华人民共和国与圭亚那共和国建交四十周年纪念封
The 40th Anniversary of the Establishment of Diplomatic Relations between the People's Republic of China and the Republic of Guyana — Commemorative Cover
2012 年 6 月 27 日发行

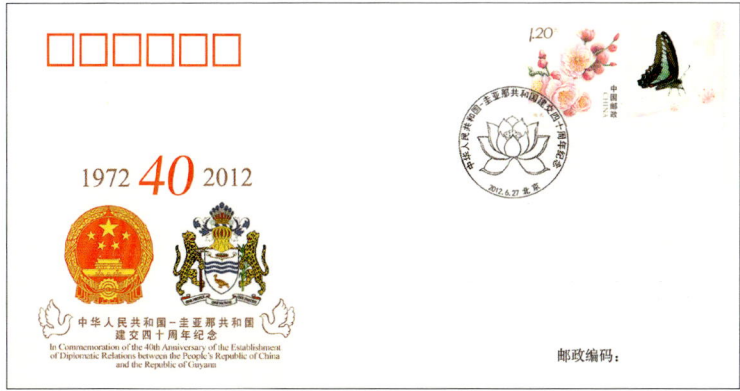

贴票：个 23《花卉》专用邮票 10 种随机贴用
信封规格：220mm×110mm
纪念封、戳设计：马小玲
发行量：80 000 枚

附：加贴圭亚那邮票（多种随机贴用）纪念活动用封

PFTN·WJ2012-30
古巴共和国国务委员会兼部长会议主席劳尔·卡斯特罗·鲁斯对中华人民共和国进行国事访问纪念封
The State Visit to the People's Republic of China by H.E. Raul Castro Ruz, President of the Council of State of Cuba and the President of the Council of Ministers of Cuba — Commemorative Cover
2012 年 7 月 4 日发行

贴票：个 19《国旗》1 枚
信封规格：220mm×110mm
纪念封、戳设计：马小玲
发行量：80 000 枚

164

PFTN·WJ2012-31
中华人民共和国与多哥共和国建交四十周年纪念封
The 40th Anniversary of the Establishment of Diplomatic Relations between the People's Republic of China and the Republic of Togo — Commemorative Cover
2012年9月19日发行

贴票：个23《花卉》专用邮票10种随机贴用
信封规格：220mm×110mm
纪念封、戳设计：马小玲
发行量：80 000枚
注：另有同图无编号纪念封，见WH-50。

附：加贴多哥邮票（3种随机贴用）的纪念活动用封

PFTN·WJ2012-32
中华人民共和国与德意志联邦共和国建交四十周年纪念封
The 40th Anniversary of the Establishment of Diplomatic Relations between the People's Republic of China and the Federal Republic of Germany — Commemorative Cover
2012 年 10 月 11 日发行

贴票：2012-20《民间传说—刘三姐》4 种随机贴用
信封规格：220mm×110mm
纪念封、戳设计：马小玲
发行量：80 000 枚
注：封面印有德国方面设计的纪念标志。

PFTN·WJ2012-33
中华人民共和国与卢森堡大公国建交四十周年纪念封
The 40th Anniversary of the Establishment of Diplomatic Relations between the People's Republic of China and the Grand Duchy of Luxembourg — Commemorative Cover
2012 年 11 月 16 日发行

贴票：2013 年贺年邮票《福临门》1 枚
信封规格：220mm×110mm
纪念封、戳设计：马小玲
发行量：80 000 枚

附：加贴卢森堡邮票的纪念活动用封

PFTN·WJ2012-34
中华人民共和国与澳大利亚联邦建交四十周年纪念封
The 40th Anniversary of the Establishment of Diplomatic Relations between the People's Republic of China and the Commonwealth of Australia — Commemorative Cover
2012年12月21日发行

贴票：2012-12《明清家具—承具》4种随机贴用
信封规格：220mm×110mm
纪念封、戳设计：马小玲
发行量：80 000枚
注：纪念活动用此封，另加盖相关戳记。

PFTN·WJ2013-1

秘鲁共和国总统奥扬塔·乌马拉·塔索对中华人民共和国进行国事访问纪念封

The State Visit to the People's Republic of China by H.E. Ollanta Humala Tasso, President of the Republic of Peru — Commemorative Cove

2013 年 4 月 5 日发行

贴票：2013-6《桃花》9 种随机贴用
信封规格：220mm×110mm
纪念封、戳设计：马小玲
发行量：50 000 枚

PFTN·WJ2013-2

乌拉圭东岸共和国总统何塞·阿尔韦托·穆希卡·科尔达诺对中华人民共和国进行工作访问纪念封

The Offical Visit to the People's Republic of China by H.E. José Alberto Mujica Cordano, President of Oriental Republic of Uruguay — Commemorative Cover

2013 年 5 月 25 日发行

贴票：2013-12《中国古镇（一）》8 种随机贴用
信封规格：220mm×110mm
纪念封、戳设计：马小玲
发行量：50 000 枚

PFTN·WJ2013-3

斯里兰卡民主社会主义共和国总统马欣达·拉贾帕克萨对中华人民共和国进行国事访问纪念封
The State Visit to the People's Republic of China by H.E. Mahinda Rajapasksa, President of the Democratic Socialist Republic of Sri Lanka — Commemorative Cover
2013 年 5 月 27 日发行

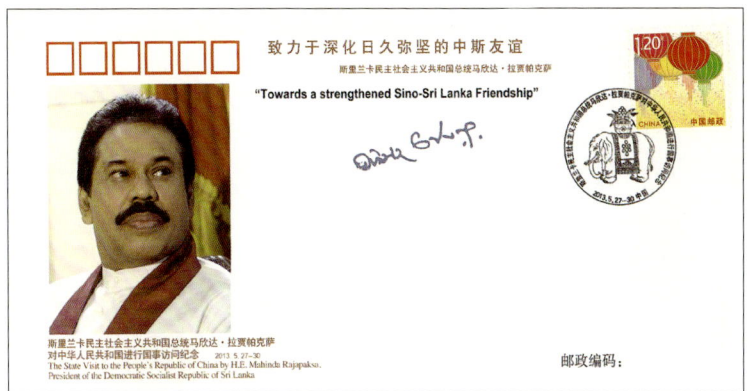

贴票：个 27《张灯结彩》1 枚
信封规格：220mm×110mm
纪念封、戳设计：马小玲
发行量：50 000 枚

PFTN·WJ2013-4

尼日利亚联邦共和国总统古德勒克·乔纳森对中华人民共和国进行国事访问纪念封
The State Visit to the People's Republic of China by H.E. Goodluck Jonathan, President of the Federal Republic of Nigeria — Commemorative Cover
2013 年 7 月 9 日发行

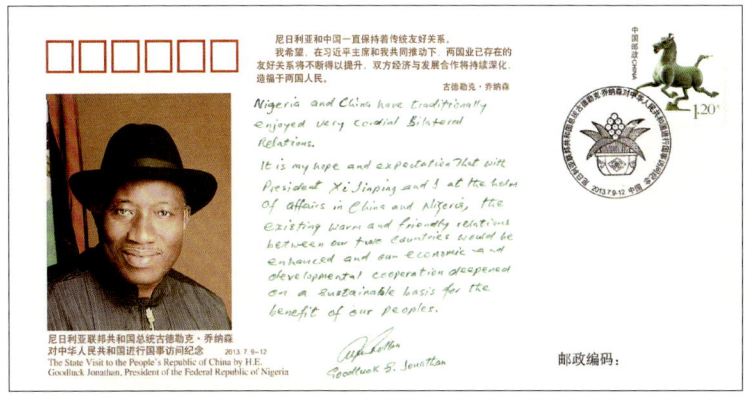

贴票：个 28《马踏飞燕》1 枚
信封规格：220mm×110mm
纪念封、戳设计：马小玲
发行量：50 000 枚

PFTN·WJ2013-5
中华人民共和国与柬埔寨王国建交五十五周年纪念封
The 55th Anniversary of the Establishment of Diplomatic Relations between the People's Republic of China and Kingdom of Cambodia — Commemorative Cover
2013 年 7 月 19 日发行

贴票：2013-14《金铜佛造像》5 种随机贴用
信封规格：220mm×110mm
纪念封、戳设计：马小玲
发行量：50 000 枚

附：加贴柬埔寨邮票（2 种随机贴用）纪念活动用封

PFTN·WJ2013-6
肯尼亚共和国总统乌胡鲁·肯雅塔对中华人民共和国进行国事访问纪念封
The State Visit to the People's Republic of China by H.E. Uhuru Kenyatta, President of the Republic of Kenya — Commemorative Cover
2013 年 8 月 18 日发行

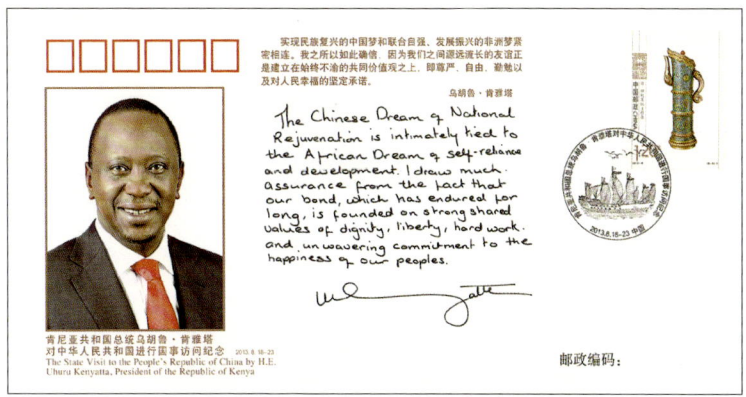

贴票：2013-9《景泰蓝》4 种随机贴用。有加贴肯尼亚邮票的纪念活动用封。
信封规格：220mm×110mm
纪念封、戳设计：马小玲
发行量：50 000 枚

PFTN·WJ2013-7
中华人民共和国与马其顿共和国建交二十周年纪念封
The 20th Anniversary of the Establishment of Diplomatic Relations between the People's Republic of China and the Republic of Macedonia — Commemorative Cover
2013 年 10 月 12 日发行

贴票：2014 年贺年专用邮票《春》1 枚
信封规格：220mm×110mm
纪念封、戳设计：马小玲
发行量：50 000 枚

附：加贴马其顿邮票的纪念活动用封

PFTN·WJ2013-8
加拿大总督戴维·约翰斯顿对中华人民共和国进行国事访问纪念封
The State Visit to the People's Republic of China by H.E. the Right Honourable David Johnston, Governor General of Canada — Commemorative Cover
2013年10月18日发行

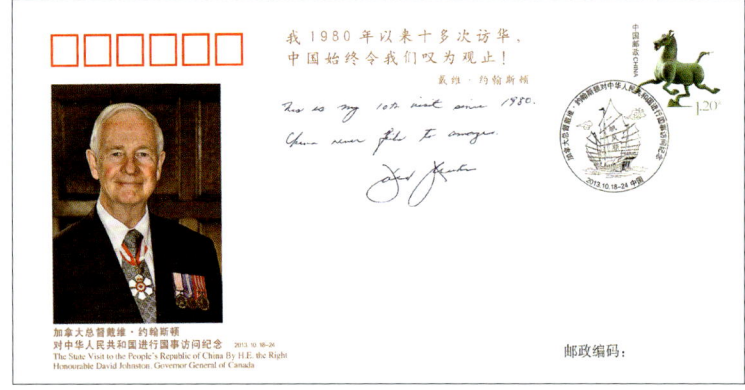

贴票：个28《马踏飞燕》1枚。有加贴加拿大邮票（多种随机贴用）纪念活动用封。
信封规格：220mm×110mm
纪念封、戳设计：马小玲
发行量：50 000枚

PFTN·WJ2013-9
中华人民共和国与汤加王国建交十五周年纪念封
The 15th Anniversary of the Establishment of Diplomatic Relations between the People's Republic of China and the Kingdom of Tonga — Commemorative Cover
2013 年 11 月 2 日发行

贴票：2014-15《琴棋书画》4 种随机贴用。有加贴汤加邮票（5 种随机贴用）纪念活动用封。
信封规格：220mm×110mm
纪念封、戳设计：马小玲
发行量：50 000 枚

PFTN·WJ2013-10
也门共和国总统阿卜杜拉布·曼苏尔·哈迪对中华人民共和国进行国事访问纪念封
The State Visit to the People's Republic of China by H.E. Abdullah Bbu Mansoor Hardy, President of the Republic of Yemen — Commemorative Cover
2013 年 11 月 12 日发行

贴票：贺卡专用邮票《流光溢彩》1 枚
信封规格：220mm×110mm
纪念封、戳设计：马小玲
发行量：50 000 枚

PFTN·WJ2013-11

乌克兰总统维克托·费奥多罗维奇·亚努科维奇对中华人民共和国进行国事访问纪念封
The State Visit to the People's Republic of China by H.E. Viktor Fedorovych Yanukovych, President of the Ukraine — Commemorative Cover
2013 年 12 月 3 日发行

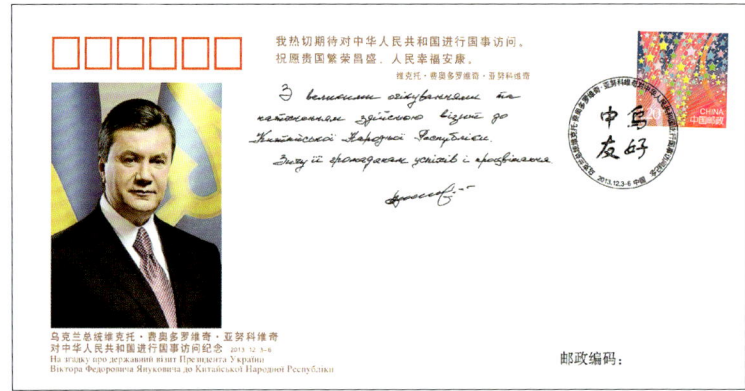

贴票：贺卡专用邮票《流光溢彩》1 枚
信封规格：220mm×110mm
纪念封、戳设计：马小玲
发行量：50 000 枚

附：加贴乌克兰邮票（多种随机贴用）纪念活动用封

PFTN·WJ2013-12
中华人民共和国与肯尼亚建交五十周年纪念封
The 50th Anniversary of the Establishment of Diplomatic Relations between the People's Republic of China and the Republic of Kenya — Commemorative Cover
2013 年 12 月 14 日发行

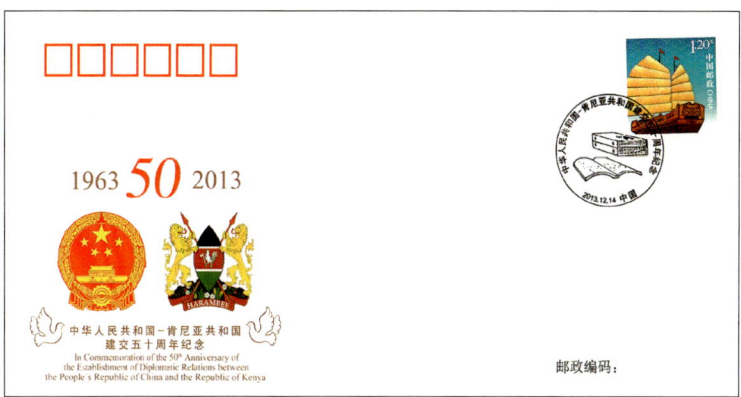

贴票：个 31《一帆风顺》个性化专用邮票 1 枚
信封规格：220mm×110mm
纪念封、戳设计：马小玲
发行量：50 000 枚

附：加贴肯尼亚邮票（2 种随机贴用）纪念活动用封

PFTN·WJ2013-13

中华人民共和国与阿尔及利亚建交五十五周年纪念封
The 55th Anniversary of the Establishment of Diplomatic Relations between the People's Republic of China and the People's Democratic Republic of Algeria — Commemorative Cover
2013年12月20日发行

贴票：2012-19《丝绸之路》4种随机贴用
信封规格：220mm×110mm
纪念封、戳设计：马小玲
发行量：50 000枚

附：加贴阿尔及利亚邮票的纪念活动用封

PFTN·WJ2013-14
多民族玻利维亚国总统胡安·埃沃·莫拉莱斯·艾马对中华人民共和国进行国事访问纪念封
The State Visit to the People's Republic of China by H.E. Juan Evo Moreles Ayma, President of the Multinational States of Bolivia — Commemorative Cover
2013 年 12 月 19 日发行

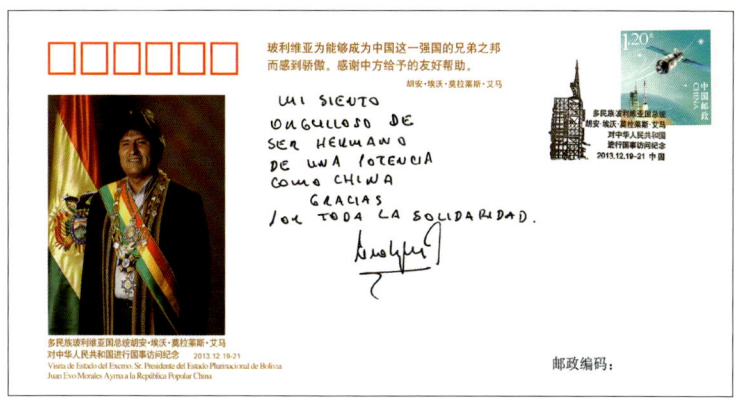

贴票：个 24《航天》1 枚
信封规格：220mm×110mm
纪念封、戳设计：马小玲
发行量：50 000 枚

4. 外交系列特种纪念封无编号
（WH-1—WH-61）
2004年2月至2013年5月发行

WH-1
中华人民共和国与葡萄牙共和国建交二十五周年纪念封
The 25th Anniversary of the Establishment of Diplomatic Relations between the People's Republic of China and the Portuguese Republic — Commemorative Cover
2004年2月8日发行

贴票：特5-2003《中国首次载人航天飞行成功》邮票2种随机贴用。葡萄牙邮票1种。
信封规格：208mm×110mm
纪念封、戳设计：马小玲
发行量：2 000枚

WH-2

中华人民共和国与委内瑞拉玻利瓦尔共和国建交三十周年纪念封
The 30th Anniversary of the Establishment of Diplomatic Relations between the People's Republic of China and the Bolivarian Republic of Venezuela — Commemorative Cover
2004 年 6 月 28 日发行

贴票：2004-5《成语典故（一）》4 种、委内瑞拉邮票 8 种随机贴用。
信封规格：208mm×110mm
纪念封、戳设计：马小玲
发行量：3 000 枚

WH-3

中华人民共和国与加蓬共和国建交三十周年纪念封
The 30th Anniversary of the Establishment of Diplomatic Relations between the People's Republic of China and the Gabonese Republic — Commemorative Cover
全套丝绸纪念封 2 枚
2-1：2004 年 4 月 20 日发行
2-2：2004 年 9 月 7 日发行

（2-1）

（2-2）

贴票：2-1：加蓬邮票 2 枚。
      2-2：1999-11《中华人民共和国成立 50 周年—民族大团结》56 种随机贴用。
信封规格：230mm×120mm
纪念封、戳设计：马小玲
发行量：2 000（套）
注：封内各镶嵌加蓬木质小型张一枚。
      2-2：封面加字"加蓬共和国哈吉·奥马尔·邦戈·翁丁巴阁下对中华人民共和国进行国事访问纪念"。

WH-4
中华人民共和国与菲律宾共和国建交三十周年纪念封
The 30th Anniversary of the Establishment of Diplomatic Relations between the People's Republic of China and the Republic of the Philippines — Commemorative Cover
2005 年 6 月 9 日发行

贴票：1999-11《中华人民共和国成立 50 周年—民族大团结》56 种、菲律宾邮票 2 种随机贴用。
信封规格：220mm×110mm
纪念封、戳设计：马小玲
发行量：3 000 枚

WH-5
中华人民共和国与泰王国建交三十周年纪念封
The 30th Anniversary of the Establishment of Diplomatic Relations between the People's Republic of China and the Kingdom of Thailand — Commemorative Cover
2005 年 7 月 1 日发行

贴票：个 6《花开富贵》加印"中泰友谊"附票 4 种、泰国邮票 2 种随机贴用。
信封规格：220mm×110mm
纪念封、戳设计：马小玲
发行量：2 000 枚

WH-6
中华人民共和国与毛里塔尼亚伊斯兰共和国建交四十周年纪念封
The 40th Anniversary of the Establishment of Diplomatic Relations between the People's Republic of China and the Islamic Republic of Mauritania — Commemorative Cover
2005 年 7 月 19 日发行

贴票：1999-11《中华人民共和国成立 50 周年—民族大团结》56 种、毛里塔尼亚邮票 2 种随机贴用。
信封规格：220mm×110mm
纪念封、戳设计：马小玲
发行量：2 000 枚

WH-7
中华人民共和国与津巴布韦共和国建交二十五周年纪念封
The 25th Anniversary of the Establishment of Diplomatic Relations between the People's Republic of China and the Republic of Zimbabwe — Commemorative Cover
2005 年 7 月 26 日发行

贴票：个 5《天安门》，或个 8《长城》专用邮票 1 枚。津巴布韦邮票 2 种随机贴用。
信封规格：220mm×110mm
纪念封、戳设计：马小玲
津巴布韦纪念戳设计：吉迪恩·圣·马哈卡
发行量：2 000 枚
注：中国邮票以"津巴布韦总统罗伯特·加布里埃尔·穆加贝对中华人民共和国进行国事访问纪念"邮戳盖销。

WH-8
中华人民共和国与奥地利共和国建交三十五周年纪念封
The 35th Anniversary of the Establishment of Diplomatic Relations between the People's Republic of China and the Republic of Austria — Commemorative Cover
2006 年 5 月 28 日发行

贴票：2005-6《世界地球日》1 枚。奥地利邮票 1 种。
信封规格：220mm×110mm
纪念封、戳设计：马小玲
发行量：2 000 枚

WH-9
中华人民共和国与苏里南共和国建交三十周年纪念封
The 30th Anniversary of the Establishment of Diplomatic Relations between the People's Republic of China and the Republic of Suriname — Commemorative Cover
2006 年 5 月 28 日发行

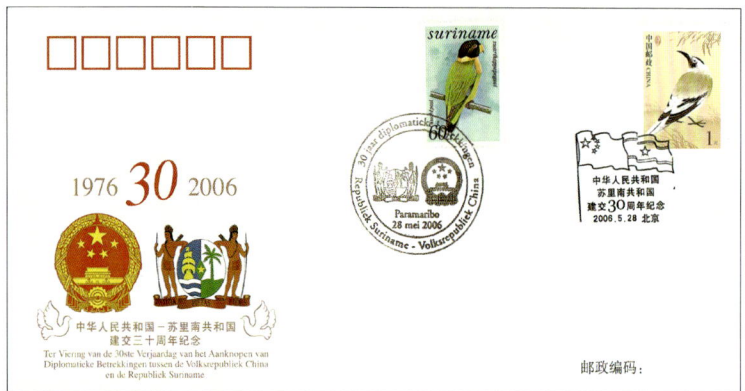

贴票：普 30《中国鸟》1 元或 2 元 1 枚。苏里南邮票 1 种。
信封规格：220mm×110mm
纪念封、戳设计：马小玲
发行量：2 000 枚

WH-10
中华人民共和国与阿拉伯埃及共和国建交五十周年纪念封
The 50th Anniversary of the Establishment of Diplomatic Relations between the People's Republic of China and the Arab Republic of Egypt — Commemorative Cover
2006 年 5 月 30 日发行

贴票：2001-20《古代金面罩头像》2 种、埃及邮票 2 种随机贴用。
信封规格：220mm×110mm
纪念封、戳设计：马小玲
发行量：2 000 枚
注：与此封同图编号外交纪念封，见 PFTN·WJ(C)-1。

WH-11
中华人民共和国与马拉维共和国建交周年纪念封
The 1st Anniversary of the Establishment of Diplomatic Relations between the People's Republic of China and the Republic of Malawi — Commemorative Cover
2008 年 12 月 28 日发行

贴票：2008-3《京剧净角》6 种随机贴用。马拉维邮票 1 种。
信封规格：220mm×110mm
纪念封、戳设计：马小玲
发行量：2 000 枚

WH-12
中华人民共和国与葡萄牙共和国建交三十周年纪念封
The 30th Anniversary of the Establishment of Diplomatic Relations between the People's Republic of China and the Portuguese Republic — Commemorative Cover
2009 年 2 月 8 日发行

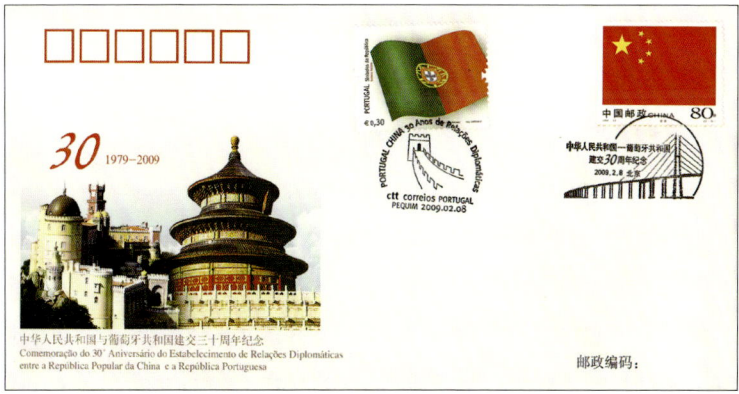

贴票：2004-23《国旗国徽》"国旗" 1 枚。葡萄牙邮票 1 种。
信封规格：220mm×110mm
纪念封、戳设计：马小玲
发行量：2 000 枚

WH-13
中华人民共和国与俄罗斯联邦建交六十周年纪念封
The 60th Anniversary of the Establishment of Diplomatic Relations between the People's Republic of China and the Russian Federation — Commemorative Cover
2009 年 10 月 2 日发行

贴票：个 19《国旗》1 枚。俄罗斯邮票 2 种随机贴用。
信封规格：220mm×110mm
纪念封、戳设计：马小玲
发行量：2 000 枚

WH-14
中华人民共和国与保加利亚共和国建交六十周年纪念封
The 60th Anniversary of the Establishment of Diplomatic Relations between the People's Republic of China and the Republic of Bulgaria — Commemorative Cover
2009 年 10 月 4 日发行

贴票：个 6《花开富贵》专用邮票 1 枚。保加利亚邮票 2 种随机贴用。
信封规格：220mm×110mm
纪念封、戳设计：马小玲
发行量：2 000 枚

WH-15
中华人民共和国与罗马尼亚建交六十周年纪念封
The 60th Anniversary of the Establishment of Diplomatic Relations between the People's Republic of China and Romania — Commemorative Cover
2009 年 10 月 5 日发行

贴票：2004-22《陶器与漆器》2 种随机贴用。罗马尼亚邮票 1 种。
信封规格：220mm×110mm
纪念封、戳设计：马小玲
发行量：2 000 枚

WH-16
中华人民共和国与捷克共和国建交六十周年纪念封
The 60th Anniversary of the Establishment of Diplomatic Relations between the People's Republic of China and the Czech Republic — Commemorative Cover
2009 年 10 月 6 日发行

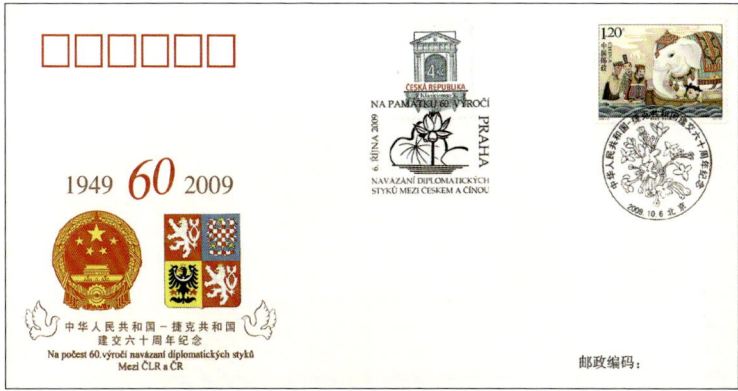

贴票：2008-13《曹冲称象》2 种随机贴用。捷克邮票 1 种。
信封规格：220mm×110mm
纪念封、戳设计：马小玲
发行量：2 000 枚

WH-17
中华人民共和国与斯洛伐克共和国建交六十周年纪念封
The 60th Anniversary of the Establishment of Diplomatic Relations between the People's Republic of China and the Slovak Republic — Commemorative Cover
2009 年 10 月 6 日发行

贴票：2002-22《亭台与城堡》2 种随机贴用。斯洛伐克邮票 1 种。
信封规格：220mm×110mm
纪念封、戳设计：马小玲
发行量：2 000 枚

WH-18
中华人民共和国与匈牙利共和国建交六十周年纪念封
The 60th Anniversary of the Establishment of Diplomatic Relations between the People's Republic of China and the Republic of Hungary — Commemorative Cover
2009 年 10 月 6 日发行

贴票：2003-19《图书艺术》2 种、匈牙利邮票 2 种随机贴用。
信封规格：220mm×110mm
纪念封、戳设计：马小玲
发行量：2 000 枚

WH-19
中华人民共和国与波兰共和国建交六十周年纪念封
The 60th Anniversary of the Establishment of Diplomatic Relations between the People's Republic of China and the Republic of Poland — Commemorative Cover
2009 年 10 月 7 日发行

贴票：2006-18《金银器》2 种随机贴用。波兰邮票 1 种。
信封规格：220mm×110mm
纪念封、戳设计：马小玲
发行量：2 000 枚

WH-20
中华人民共和国与阿尔巴尼亚共和国建交六十周年纪念封
The 60th Anniversary of the Establishment of Diplomatic Relations between the People's Republic of China and the Republic of Albania — Commemorative Cover
2009 年 11 月 23 日发行

贴票：2009-15《人民大会堂》2 种随机贴用。阿尔巴尼亚邮票 1 种。
信封规格：220mm×110mm
纪念封、戳设计：马小玲
发行量：2 000 枚

WH-21

奥地利总统海因茨·菲舍尔对中华人民共和国进行国事访问纪念封
The State Visit to the People's Republic of China by H.E. Heinz Fischer, President of the Republic of Austria — Commemorative Cover
2010 年 1 月 19 日发行

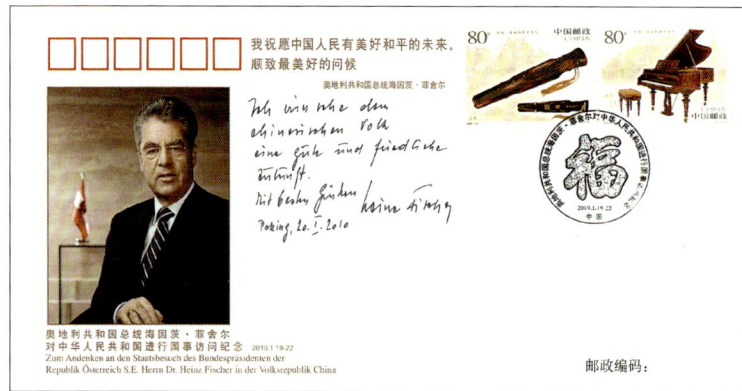

贴票：2006-22《古琴与钢琴》2 枚
信封规格：220mm×110mm
纪念封、戳设计：马小玲
发行量：2 000 枚

WH-22

中华人民共和国与哥伦比亚共和国建交三十周年纪念封
The 30th Anniversary of the Establishment of Diplomatic Relations between the People's Republic of China and the Republic of Columbia — Commemorative Cover
2010 年 2 月 7 日发行

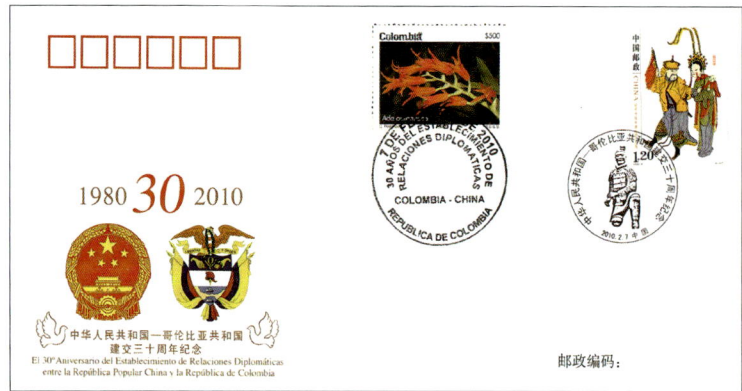

贴票：2010-4《梁平木版年画》4 种、哥伦比亚邮票 4 种随机贴用。
信封规格：220mm×110mm
纪念封、戳设计：马小玲
发行量：2 000 枚

WH-23
中华人民共和国与印度共和国建交六十周年纪念封
The 60th Anniversary of the Establishment of Diplomatic Relations between the People's Republic of China and the Republic of India — Commemorative Cover
2010 年 4 月 1 日发行

贴票：2008-7《白马寺与大菩提寺》2 枚
信封规格：220mm×110mm
纪念封、戳设计：马小玲
发行量：2 000 枚

WH-24
中华人民共和国与波斯尼亚和黑塞哥维那建交十五周年纪念封
The 15th Anniversary of the Establishment of Diplomatic Relations between the People's Republic of China and Bosnia and Herzegovina — Commemorative Cover
2010 年 4 月 3 日发行

贴票：2009 年贺年专用邮票《花开富贵》1 枚。波黑邮票 3 种随机贴用。
信封规格：220mm×110mm
纪念封、戳设计：马小玲
发行量：2 000 枚

WH-25
中华人民共和国与印度尼西亚共和国建交六十周年暨中印尼友好年纪念封
The 60th Anniversary of the Establishment of Diplomatic Relations between the People's Republic of China and the Republic of Indonesia and the Year of Friendship between China and Indonesia — Commemorative Cover
2010 年 4 月 13 日发行
全套纪念封 3 枚

(3-1)

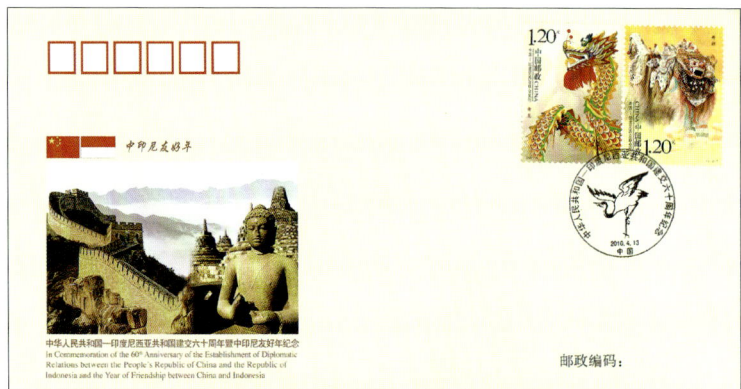

(3-2)

(3-3)

贴票：各贴2007-8《舞龙舞狮》2枚
信封规格：220mm×110mm
纪念封、戳设计：马小玲
发行量：2 000（套）

WH-26
中华人民共和国与津巴布韦共和国建交三十周年纪念封
The 30th Anniversary of the Establishment of Diplomatic Relations between the People's Republic of China and the Republic of Zimbabwe — Commemorative Cover
2010年4月18日发行

贴票：2010-1《庚寅年》1枚。津巴布韦邮票4种随机贴用。
信封规格：220mm×110mm
纪念封、戳设计：马小玲
发行量：5 000枚

WH-27
中华人民共和国与欧洲联盟建交三十五周年纪念封
The 35th Anniversary of the Establishment of Diplomatic Relations between the People's Republic of China and the European Union — Commemorative Cover
2010 年 5 月 6 日发行
全套纪念封 2 枚

(2-1)

(2-2)

贴票：2-1：个 6《花开富贵》2 枚。
　　　2-2：个 9《五福临门》2 枚。
信封规格：220mm×110mm
纪念封、戳设计：马小玲
发行量：1 500（套）

194

WH-28
中华人民共和国与缅甸联邦建交六十周年纪念封
The 60th Anniversary of the Establishment of Diplomatic Relations between the People's Republic of China and the Republic of the Union of Myanmar — Commemorative Cover
2010 年 6 月 8 日发行

贴票：个 4《一帆风顺》2 枚。缅甸邮票 1 种。
信封规格：220mm×110mm
纪念封、戳设计：马小玲
发行量：2 000 枚

WH-29
中华人民共和国与菲律宾共和国建交三十五周年纪念封
The 35th Anniversary of the Establishment of Diplomatic Relations between the People's Republic of China and the Republic of the Philippines — Commemorative Cover
2010 年 6 月 9 日发行

贴票：2008-4《中国鸟》6 种、菲律宾邮票 16 种随机贴用。
信封规格：220mm×110mm
纪念封、戳设计：马小玲
发行量：2 000 枚

WH-30
中华人民共和国与泰王国建交三十五周年纪念封
The 35th Anniversary of the Establishment of Diplomatic Relations between the People's Republic of China and the Kingdom of Thailand — Commemorative Cover
2010年7月1日发行

贴票：2009-7《中国2009世界集邮展览》2种、泰国邮票多种随机贴用。
信封规格：220mm×110mm
纪念封、戳设计：马小玲
发行量：2 000枚

WH-31
中华人民共和国与加纳共和国建交五十周年纪念封
The 50th Anniversary of the Establishment of Diplomatic Relations between the People's Republic of China and the Republic of Ghana — Commemorative Cover
2010年7月5日发行
全套纪念封2枚

(2-1)

(2-2)

贴票：2008-13《曹冲称象》2种、加纳邮票4种随机贴用。
信封规格：220mm×110mm
纪念封、戳设计：马小玲
发行量：2 000（套）

WH-32
中华人民共和国与沙特阿拉伯王国建交二十周年纪念封
The 20th Anniversary of the Establishment of Diplomatic Relations between the People's Republic of China and Kingdom of Saudi Arabia — Commemorative Cover
2010年7月21日发行

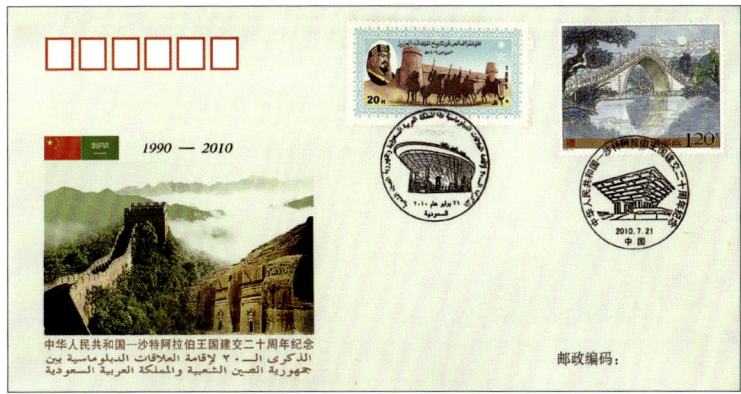

贴票：2008-10《颐和园》6种、沙特阿拉伯邮票4种随机贴用。
信封规格：220mm×110mm
纪念封、戳设计：马小玲
发行量：6 000 枚

WH-33

中华人民共和国与古巴共和国建交五十周年纪念封
The 50th Anniversary of the Establishment of Diplomatic Relations between the People's Republic of China and the Republic of Cuba — Commemorative Cover
2010 年 9 月 28 日发行

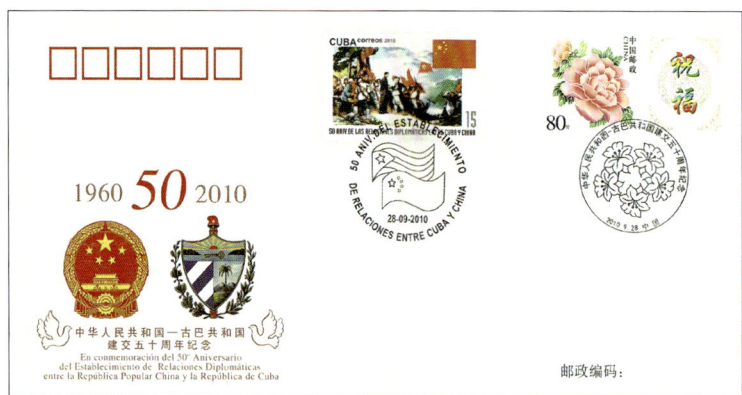

贴票：个 6《花开富贵》专用邮票 1 枚。古巴邮票 4 种随机贴用。
信封规格：220mm×110mm
纪念封、戳设计：马小玲
发行量：5 000 枚

WH-34

中华人民共和国与新加坡共和国建交二十周年纪念封
The 20th Anniversary of the Establishment of Diplomatic Relations between the People's Republic of China and the Republic of Singapore — Commemorative Cover
2010 年 10 月 3 日发行

贴票：个 6《花开富贵》1 枚。新加坡邮票 1 种。
信封规格：220mm×110mm
摄影：马驭
纪念封、戳设计：马小玲
发行量：2 000 枚

WH-35
中华人民共和国与孟加拉人民共和国建交三十五周年纪念封
The 35th Anniversary of the Establishment of Diplomatic Relations between the People's Republic of China and the People's Republic of Bangladesh — Commemorative Cover
2010 年 10 月 4 日发行

贴票：2010-1《庚寅年》1 枚。孟加拉邮票 1 种。
信封规格：220mm×110mm
纪念封、戳设计：马小玲
发行量：2 000 枚

WH-36
中华人民共和国与赤道几内亚共和国建交四十周年纪念封
The 40th Anniversary of the Establishment of Diplomatic Relations between the People's Republic of China and the Republic of Equatorial Guinea — Commemorative Cover
2010 年 10 月 15 日发行

贴票：2010-14《昆曲》3 种随机贴用。赤道几内亚邮票 1 种。
信封规格：220mm×110mm
纪念封、戳设计：马小玲
发行量：2 000 枚

WH-37
意大利共和国总统乔治·纳波利塔诺对中华人民共和国进行国事访问纪念封
The State Visit to the People's Republic of China by H.E. Giorgio Napolitano, President of Republic of Italy — Commemorative Cover
2010 年 10 月 24 日发行

贴票：个 9《五福临门》2 枚
信封规格：220mm×110mm
纪念封、戳设计：马小玲
发行量：2 000 枚

WH-38
中华人民共和国与意大利共和国建交四十周年纪念封
The 40th Anniversary of the Establishment of Diplomatic Relations between the People's Republic of China and the Republic of Italy — Commemorative Cover
2010 年 11 月 6 日发行

贴票：2008-3《京剧净角》6 种随机贴用
信封规格：220mm×110mm
纪念封、戳设计：马小玲
发行量：2 000 枚

WH-39
中华人民共和国与智利共和国建交四十周年纪念封
The 40th Anniversary of the Establishment of Diplomatic Relations between the People's Republic of China and Republic of Chile — Commemorative Cover
2010年12月15日发行

贴票：2009-2《漳州木版年画》4种、智利邮票多种随机贴用。
信封规格：220mm×110mm
纪念封、戳设计：马小玲
发行量：2 000 枚

WH-40
中华人民共和国与尼日利亚联邦共和国建交四十周年纪念封
The 40th Anniversary of the Establishment of Diplomatic Relations between the People's Republic of China and the Federal Republic of Nigeria — Commemorative Cover
2011年2月10日发行
全套纪念封2枚

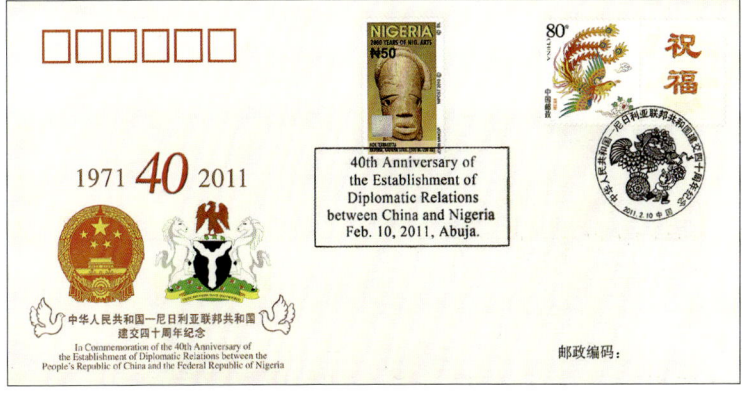

(2-1)

(2-2)

贴票：2-1：个7《吉祥如意》专用邮票1枚。尼日利亚邮票1种。
　　　2-2：2011-1《辛卯年》1枚。尼日利亚邮票1种。
信封规格：220mm×110mm
纪念封、戳设计：马小玲
发行量：2 000（套）

WH-41
中华人民共和国与科威特国建交四十周年纪念封
The 40th Anniversary of the Establishment of Diplomatic Relations between the People's Republic of China and the State of Kuwait — Commemorative Cover
2011年3月22日发行

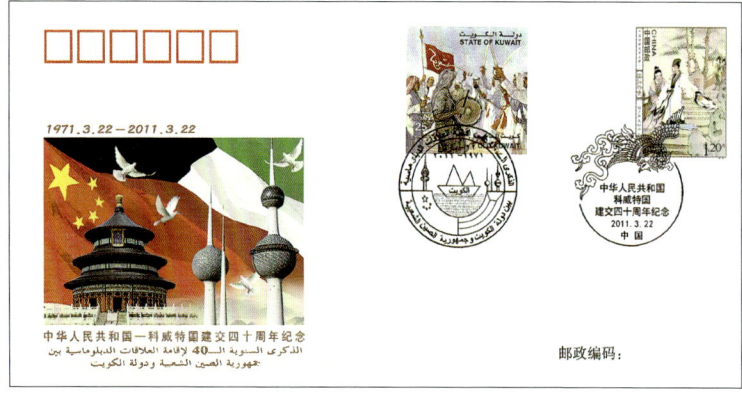

贴票：2011-5《儒林外史》6种随机贴用。科威特邮票1种。
信封规格：220mm×110mm
纪念封、戳设计：马小玲
发行量：2 000枚

WH-42
中华人民共和国与喀麦隆共和国建交四十周年纪念封
The 40th Anniversary of the Establishment of Diplomatic Relations between the People's Republic of China and the Republic of Cameroon — Commemorative Cover
2011年3月26日发行

贴票：个17《和谐》专用邮票1枚。喀麦隆邮票4种随机贴用。
信封规格：220mm×110mm
纪念封、戳设计：马小玲
发行量：2 000枚

WH-43
中华人民共和国驻蒙特利尔总领事馆开馆纪念封
In commemoration of the official opening of the Consulate General of the People's Republic of China in Montreal — Commemorative Cover
2011年6月22日发行

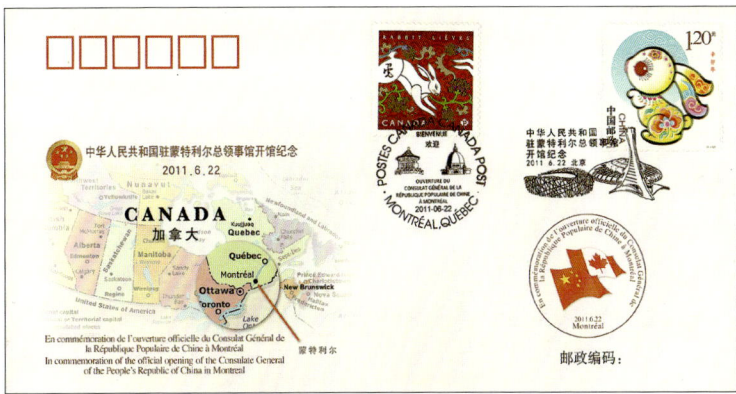

贴票：2011-1《辛卯年》1枚。加拿大邮票1种。
信封规格：220mm×110mm
纪念封、戳设计：马小玲
发行量：2 000枚

WH-44
亨利·基辛格博士访华四十周年纪念封
The 40th Anniversary of Dr. Henry Kissinger's Visit to China — Commemorative Cover
2011 年 7 月 9 日发行

贴票：2009-15《人民大会堂》2 种随机贴用。
信封规格：220mm×110mm
纪念封、戳设计：马小玲
发行量：2 000 枚
注：此封由外交部集邮协会制作。

WH-45
中华人民共和国与希腊共和国建交四十周年纪念封
The 40th Anniversary of the Establishment of Diplomatic Relations between the People's Republic of China and the Hellenic Republic — Commemorative Cover
2012 年 6 月 5 日发行

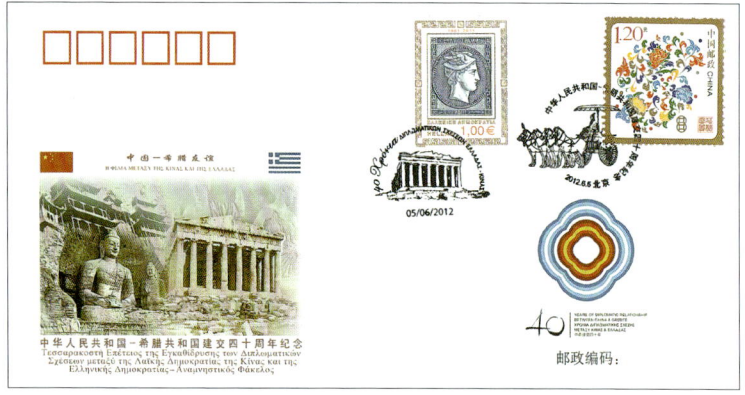

贴票：2009 年贺年专用邮票《花开富贵》1 枚。希腊邮票 1 种。
信封规格：220mm×110mm
纪念封、戳设计：马小玲
希腊纪念戳设计：罗丹希·森珠卡
发行量：2 000 枚
注：封面印有希腊方面设计的纪念标志。

WH-46

俄罗斯联邦总统弗拉基米尔·弗拉基米洛维奇·普京对中华人民共和国进行国事访问并出席上海合作组织成员国元首理事会第十二次会议纪念封

The State Visit to the People's Republic of China by H.E. Vladimir Vladimirovich Putin, President of the Russian Federation and to attend the Shanghai Cooperation Organization, the Twelfth Meeting of the Council of heads of Member States — Commemorative Cover

2012年6月5日发行

贴票：个19《国旗》1枚
信封规格：220mm×110mm
纪念封、戳设计：马小玲
发行量：2 000枚

WH-47

哥斯达黎加共和国总统劳拉·钦奇利亚·米兰达对中华人民共和国进行国事访问纪念封

The State Visit to the People's Republic of China by H.E. Laura Chinchilla Miranda, President of the Republic of Costa Rica — Commemorative Cover

2012年8月12日发行

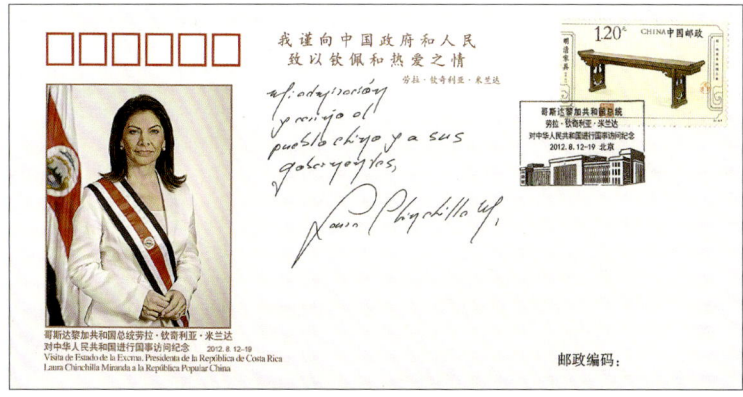

贴票：2012-12《明清家具—承具》4种随机贴用
信封规格：220mm×110mm
纪念封、戳设计：马小玲
发行量：2 000枚

WH-48

中华人民共和国与大韩民国建交二十周年暨中韩友好交流年纪念封
The 20th Anniversary of the Establishment of Diplomatic Relations between the People's Republic of China and the Republic of Korea, and China-the Republic of Korea Friendly Exchange Year — Commemorative Cover
2012年8月24日发行

贴票：个23《花卉》专用邮票10种随机贴用。有加盖相关戳记的纪念活动用封。
信封规格：220mm×110mm
纪念封、戳设计：马小玲
发行量：2 000 枚

WH-49

中国—中东欧国家合作秘书处成立大会暨首次国家协调员会议纪念封
The Inaugural Conference of the Secretariat for Cooperation between China and Central and Eastern European Countries & the First National Coordinators' Meeting — Commemorative Cover
2012年9月6日发行

贴票：个19《国旗》1枚
信封规格：220mm×110mm
纪念封、戳设计：马小玲、靳启铭
发行量：2 000 枚

WH-50
中华人民共和国与多哥共和国建交四十周年纪念封
The 40th Anniversary of the Establishment of Diplomatic Relations between the People's Republic of China and the Republic of Togo — Commemorative Cover
2012 年 9 月 19 日发行

贴票：2009 年贺年专用邮票《花开富贵》1 枚。多哥邮票 3 种（或小型张）随机贴用。
信封规格：220mm×110mm
纪念封、戳设计：马小玲
发行量：2 000 枚
注：与此封同图编号外交纪念封，见 PFTN·WJ2012-31。

WH-51
中华人民共和国与马尔代夫共和国建交四十周年纪念封
The 40th Anniversary of the Establishment of Diplomatic Relations between the People's Republic of China and the Republic of Maldives — Commemorative Cover
2012 年 10 月 14 日发行

贴票：个 4《一帆风顺》专用邮票 1 种、个 6《花开富贵》专用邮票 1 种，或个 23《花卉》专用邮票 10 种随机贴用。马尔代夫邮票 6 种随机贴用。
信封规格：220mm×110mm
纪念封、戳设计：马小玲
发行量：5 000 枚
注：此封由中国驻马尔代夫使馆与外交部集邮协会共同制作。

WH-52

中华人民共和国与马达加斯加共和国建交四十周年纪念封
The 40th Anniversary of the Establishment of Diplomatic Relations between the People's Republic of China and the Republic of Madagascar — Commemorative Cover
2012 年 11 月 6 日发行

贴票：2012-21《和田玉》4 种、马达加斯加邮票 2 种随机贴用。
信封规格：220mm×110mm
纪念封、戳设计：马小玲
发行量：2 000 枚
注：此封由中国驻马达加斯加使馆与外交部集邮协会共同制作。

WH-53

中华人民共和国与牙买加建交四十周年纪念封
The 40th Anniversary of the Establishment of Diplomatic Relations between the People's Republic of China and Jamaica — Commemorative Cover
2012 年 11 月 21 日发行

贴票：2012-28《中国陶瓷—德化窑瓷器》4 种随机贴用。牙买加邮票 1 种。
信封规格：220mm×110mm
纪念封、戳设计：马小玲
发行量：3 000 枚

WH-54

中国印度友好协会成立六十周年纪念封
The 60th Anniversary of the Establishment of China-India Friendship Association — Commemorative Cover
2012 年 11 月 23 日发行

贴票：2012-19《丝绸之路》4 种随机贴用
信封规格：220mm×110mm
纪念封、戳设计：马小玲
发行量：2 000 枚
注：纪念活动用此封，另加盖相关戳记。

WH-55

中华人民共和国与新西兰建交四十周年纪念封
The 40th Anniversary of the Establishment of Diplomatic Relations between the People's Republic of China and New Zealand — Commemorative Cover
2012 年 12 月 22 日发行

贴票：2013 年贺年专用邮票《福临门》1 枚。新西兰邮票 4 种随机贴用。
信封规格：220mm×110mm
纪念封、戳设计：马小玲、张帆
发行量：2 000 枚

WH-56

中华人民共和国与安提瓜和巴布达建交三十周年纪念封
The 30th Anniversary of the Establishment of Diplomatic Relations between the People's Republic of China and Antigua and Barbuda — Commemorative Cover
2013 年 1 月 1 日发行

贴票：2013 年贺年专用邮票《福临门》1 枚。安提瓜和巴布达邮票 1 种。
信封规格：220mm×110mm
纪念封、戳设计：马小玲
发行量：2 500 枚

WH-57

中华人民共和国与安哥拉共和国建交三十周年纪念封
The 30th Anniversary of the Establishment of Diplomatic Relations between the People's Republic of China and the Republic of Angola — Commemorative Cover
2013 年 1 月 12 日发行

贴票：2012-24《延边风情》3 种、安哥拉邮票 6 种随机贴用。
信封规格：220mm×110mm
纪念封、戳设计：马小玲
发行量：2 000 枚
注：此封由中国驻安哥拉使馆、安哥拉驻华使馆和外交部集邮协会联合制作。

WH-58
中华人民共和国与科特迪瓦共和国建交三十周年纪念封
The 30th Anniversary of the Establishment of Diplomatic Relations between the People's Republic of China and Republic of Cote d'Ivoire — Commemorative Cover
2013 年 3 月 2 日发行

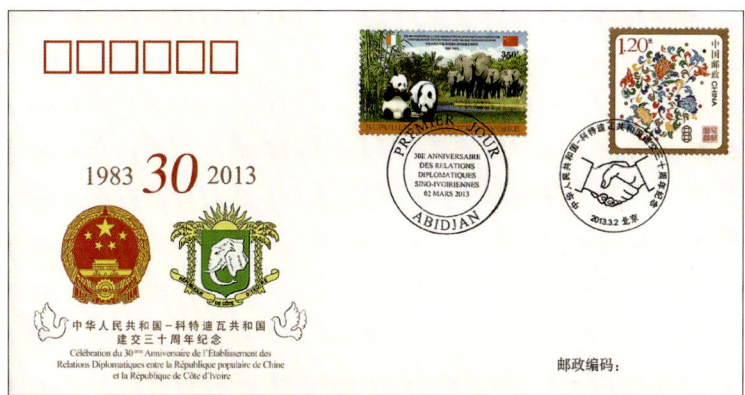

贴票：2009 年贺年专用邮票《花开富贵》1 种，或 2012-7《福禄寿喜》4 种随机贴用。科特迪瓦邮票 4 种随机贴用。
信封规格：220mm×110mm
纪念封、戳设计：马小玲
发行量：3 000 枚
注：此封由中国驻科特迪瓦使馆、科特迪瓦驻华使馆与外交部集邮协会联合制作。

WH-59
中华人民共和国与西班牙王国建交四十周年纪念封
The 40th Anniversary of the Establishment of Diplomatic Relations between the People's Republic of China and the Kingdom of Spain — Commemorative Cover
2013 年 3 月 9 日发行

贴票：个 27《张灯结彩》1 枚。西班牙邮票 1 种。
信封规格：220mm×110mm
纪念封、戳设计：马小玲
发行量：5 000 枚

WH-60

中国向阿尔及利亚暨向非洲派遣第一支医疗队五十周年纪念封

The 50th Anniversary of China to Algeria and to Africa dispatched the first medical team — Commemorative Cover

2013年4月16日发行

贴票：个26《爱》1枚。阿尔及利亚邮票或小型张随机贴用。
信封规格：220mm×110mm
纪念封、戳设计：马小玲
发行量：2 000枚
注：此封由中国驻阿尔及利亚使馆与外交部集邮协会共同制作。

WH-61

中华人民共和国与厄立特里亚国建交二十周年纪念封

The 20th Anniversary of the Establishment of Diplomatic Relations between the People's Republic of China and the State of Eritrea — Commemorative Cover

2013年5月24日发行

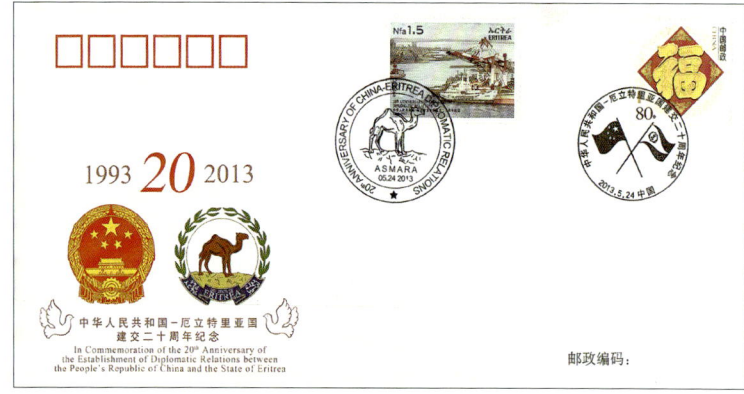

贴票：个9《五福临门》1枚。厄立特里亚邮票8种随机贴用。
信封规格：220mm×110mm
纪念封、戳设计：马小玲
发行量：3 000枚
注：此封由中国驻厄立特里亚使馆与外交部集邮协会共同制作。

附录：

各国（国际组织）与中华人民共和国建交时间及相关外交系列特种纪念封索引

一、亚洲 ASIA

国家	与中国建交日	外交纪念封编号（序号）
阿富汗伊斯兰共和国 The Islamic Republic of Afghanistan	1955.1.20	PFTN·WJ-96、PFTN·WJ-153
阿拉伯联合酋长国 The United Arab Emirates	1984.11.1	PFTN·WJ-24
阿拉伯叙利亚共和国 The Syrian Arab Republic	1956.8.1	PFTN·WJ-71、PFTN·WJ（C）-2
阿曼苏丹国 The Sultanate of Oman	1978.5.25	PFTN·WJ-131、PFTN·WJ（C）-23
阿塞拜疆共和国 The Republic of Azerbaijan	1992.4.2	PFTN·WJ-103、PFTN·WJ（C）-15、PFTN·WJ2012-15
巴基斯坦伊斯兰共和国 The Islamic Republic of Pakistan	1951.5.21	PFTN·WJ-65、PFTN·WJ（B12）-160、PFTN·WJ2011-4
巴勒斯坦国 The State of Palestine	1988.11.20	
巴林王国 The Kingdom of Bahrain	1989.4.18	PFTN·WJ-5
朝鲜民主主义人民共和国 Democratic People's Republic of Korea	1949.10.6	PFTN·WJ-18、PFTN·WJ（B6）-146、PFTN·WJ-179
大韩民国 Republic of Korea	1992.8.24	PFTN·WJ-113、PFTN·WJ（B6）-146、PFTN·WJ-179、WH-48
东帝汶民主共和国 Democratic Republic of Timor-Leste	2002.5.20	PFTN·WJ2012-22
菲律宾共和国 Republic of the Philippines	1975.6.9	PFTN·WJ-37、WH-4、WH-29
格鲁吉亚 Georgia	1992.6.9	PFTN·WJ-111、PFTN·WJ（C）-20、PFTN·WJ2012-28
哈萨克斯坦共和国 The Republic of Kazakhstan	1992.1.3	PFTN·WJ-87、PFTN·WJ（B17）-165、PFTN·WJ（C）-6、PFTN·WJ2012-2
吉尔吉斯共和国 Kyrgyz Republic	1992.1.5	PFTN·WJ-90、PFTN·WJ（C）-9、PFTN·WJ2012-5
柬埔寨王国 Kingdom of Cambodia	1958.7.19	PFTN·WJ-133、PFTN·WJ（B6）-146、PFTN·WJ2013-5
卡塔尔国 The State of Qatar	1988.7.9	PFTN·WJ-132
科威特国 The State of Kuwait	1971.3.22	PFTN·WJ-60、WH-41

国家	与中国建交日	外交纪念封编号（序号）
老挝人民民主共和国 The Lao People's Democratic Republic	1961.4.25	PFTN·WJ-62、PFTN·WJ（B6）-146、PFTN·WJ2011-2
黎巴嫩共和国 The Republic of Leabanon	1971.11.9	PFTN·WJ-82、PFTN·WJ2011-19
马尔代夫共和国 The Republic of Maldives	1972.10.14	PFTN·WJ-117、WH-51
马来西亚 Malaysia	1974.5.31	PFTN·WJ-8、PFTN·WJ（B7）-147、PFTN·WJ-177
蒙古国 Mongolia	1949.10.16	PFTN·WJ-22
孟加拉国人民共和国 The People's Republic of Bangladesh	1975.10.4	PFTN·WJ-50、PFTN·WJ（B11）-157、WH-35
缅甸联邦共和国 Republic of the Union of Myanmar	1950.6.8	PFTN·WJ-36、WH-28
尼泊尔联邦民主共和国 The Federal Democratic Republic of Nepal	1955.8.1	PFTN·WJ-45
日本国 Japan	1972.9.29	PFTN·WJ-115、PFTN·WJ-135、PFTN·WJ-179
沙特阿拉伯王国 Kingdom of Saudi Arabia	1990.7.21	PFTN·WJ-44、WH-32
斯里兰卡民主社会主义共和国 The Democratic Socialist Republic of Sri Lanka	1957.2.7	PFTN·WJ-97、PFTN·WJ2013-3
塔吉克斯坦共和国 The Republic of Tajikistan	1992.1.4	PFTN·WJ-89、PFTN·WJ（C）-8、PFTN·WJ2012-4
泰王国 The Kingdom of Thailand	1975.7.1	PFTN·WJ-40、WH-5、WH-30
土耳其共和国 Republic of Turkey	1971.8.4	PFTN·WJ-72
土库曼斯坦 Turkmenistan	1992.1.6	PFTN·WJ-91、PFTN·WJ（C）-10、PFTN·WJ2012-6
文莱达鲁萨兰国 Negara Brunei Darussalam	1991.9.30	PFTN·WJ-78、PFTN·WJ2011-16
乌兹别克斯坦共和国 The Republic of Uzbekistan	1992.1.2	PFTN·WJ-86、PFTN·WJ（C）-5、PFTN·WJ2012-1
新加坡共和国 The Republic of Singapore	1990.10.3	PFTN·WJ-49、WH-34
亚美尼亚共和国 The Republic of Armenia	1992.4.6	PFTN·WJ-104、PFTN·WJ（C）-16、PFTN·WJ2012-16
也门共和国 The Republic of Yemen	1956.9.24	PFTN·WJ-77、PFTN·WJ2013-10
伊拉克共和国 The Republic of Iraq	1958.8.25	PFTN·WJ-176
伊朗伊斯兰共和国 The Islamic Republic of Iran	1971.8.16	PFTN·WJ-73

国家	与中国建交日	外交纪念封编号（序号）
以色列国 The State of Israel	1992.1.24	PFTN·WJ-93、PFTN·WJ2012-8
印度共和国 The Republic of India	1950.4.1	PFTN·WJ-31、WH-23、WH-54
印度尼西亚共和国 Republic of Indonesia	1950.4.13	PFTN·WJ-32、WH-25
约旦哈希姆王国 The Hashemite Kingdom of Jordan	1977.4.7	PFTN·WJ-105
越南社会主义共和国 The Socialist Republic of Viet Nam	1950.1.18	PFTN·WJ-28、PFTN·WJ（B6）-146、PFTN·WJ2010-1
中华人民共和国 The People's Republic of China	—	PFTN·WJ（B8）-149、PFTN·WJ（B8）-155、PFTN·WJ（B14）-162、WH-44

二、非洲 AFRICA

国家	与中国建交日	外交纪念封编号（序号）
阿尔及利亚民主人民共和国 The People's Democratic Republic of Algeria	1958.12.20	PFTN·WJ-141、PFTN·WJ（C）-25、WH-60、PFTN·WJ2013-13
阿拉伯埃及共和国 The Arab Republic of Egypt	1956.5.30	PFTN·WJ-68、WH-10、PFTN·WJ（C）-1
埃塞俄比亚联邦民主共和国 The Federal Democratic Republic of Ethiopia	1970.11.24	PFTN·WJ-57
安哥拉共和国 The Republic of Angola	1983.1.12	PFTN·WJ-126、WH-57
贝宁共和国 The Republic of Benin	1964.11.12	PFTN·WJ-124
博茨瓦纳共和国 The Republic of Botswana	1975.1.6	PFTN·WJ-27
布隆迪共和国 The Republic of Burundi	1963.12.21	
赤道几内亚共和国 The Republic of Equatorial Guinea	1970.10.15	PFTN·WJ-158、WH-36
多哥共和国 The Republic of Togo	1972.9.19	PFTN·WJ-114、PFTN·WJ2012-31、WH-50
厄立特里亚国 The State of Eritrea	1993.5.24	PFTN·WJ-130、WH-61
佛得角共和国 The Republic of Cape Verde	1976.4.25	PFTN·WJ-63
刚果共和国 The Republic of Congo	1964.2.22	PFTN·WJ-144
刚果民主共和国 The Democratic Republic of the Congo	1961.2.20	
吉布提共和国 The Republic of Djibouti	1979.1.8	PFTN·WJ-142
几内亚共和国 The Republic of Guinea	1959.10.4	PFTN·WJ-14
几内亚（比绍）共和国 The Republic of Guinea-Bissau	1974.3.15	

国家	与中国建交日	外交纪念封编号（序号）
加纳共和国 The Republic of Ghana	1960.7.5	PFTN·WJ-41、WH-31
加蓬共和国 The Gabonese Republic	1974.4.20	PFTN·WJ-6、PFTN·WJ（B5）-145、WH-3
津巴布韦共和国 The Republic of Zimbabwe	1980.4.18	PFTN·WJ-33、WH-7、WH-26
喀麦隆共和国 The Republic of Cameroon	1971.3.26	PFTN·WJ-61、WH-42、PFTN·WJ2011-11
科摩罗联盟 Union of Comoros	1975.11.13	PFTN·WJ-159
科特迪瓦共和国 Republic of Cote d'Ivoire	1983.3.2	PFTN·WJ-128、WH-58
肯尼亚共和国 The Republic of Kenya	1963.12.14	PFTN·WJ-140、PFTN·WJ2013-6、PFTN·WJ2013-12
莱索托王国 The Kingdom of Lesotho	1983.4.30	
利比里亚共和国 The Republic of Liberia	1977.2.17	
利比亚 The Great Socialist People's Libyan Arab Jamahiriya	1978.8.9	PFTN·WJ-134
卢旺达共和国 The Republic of Rwanda	1971.11.12	PFTN·WJ-83
马达加斯加共和国 The Republic of Madagascar	1972.11.6	PFTN·WJ-119、WH-52
马拉维共和国 The Republic of Malawi	2007.12.28	WH-11
马里共和国 The Republic of Mali	1960.10.25	PFTN·WJ-52
毛里求斯共和国 The Republic of Mauritius	1972.4.15	PFTN·WJ-106、PFTN·WJ2012-17
毛里塔尼亚伊斯兰共和国 The Islamic Republic of Mauritania	1965.7.19	PFTN·WJ-43、WH-6
摩洛哥王国 The Kingdom of Morocco	1958.11.1	PFTN·WJ-138、PFTN·WJ（C）-24
莫桑比克共和国 The Republic of Mozambique	1975.6.25	PFTN·WJ-38
纳米比亚共和国 The Republic of Namibia	1990.3.22	PFTN·WJ-30、PFTN·WJ2010-3
南非共和国 The Republic of South Africa	1998.1.1	PFTN·WJ-169
南苏丹共和国 The Republic of South Sudan	2011.7.9	PFTN·WJ2011-8、PFTN·WJ2012-18
尼日尔共和国 The Republic of Niger	1974.7.20	
尼日利亚联邦共和国 The Federal Republic of Nigeria	1971.2.10	PFTN·WJ-59、WH-40、PFTN·WJ2013-4
塞拉利昂共和国 The Republic of Sierra Leone	1971.7.29	PFTN·WJ-70、PFTN·WJ2011-12
塞内加尔共和国 The Republic of Senegal	1971.12.7	

国家	与中国建交日	外交纪念封编号（序号）
塞舌尔共和国 Republic of Seychelles	1976.6.30	PFTN·WJ-69
苏丹共和国 The Republic of the Sudan	1959.2.4	PFTN·WJ-3、PFTN·WJ（C）-27
索马里联邦共和国 The Somali Republic	1960.12.14	
坦桑尼亚联合共和国 The United Republic of Tanzania	1964.4.26	PFTN·WJ-7
突尼斯共和国 The Republic of Tunisia	1964.1.10	PFTN·WJ-143
乌干达共和国 The Republic of Uganda	1962.10.18	PFTN·WJ-118
赞比亚共和国 The Republic of Zambia	1964.10.29	PFTN·WJ-23
乍得共和国 The Republic of Chad	1972.11.28	
中非共和国 The Central Africa Republic	1964.9.29	

三、欧洲 EUROPE

国家	与中国建交日	外交纪念封编号（序号）
阿尔巴尼亚共和国 The Republic of Albania	1949.11.23	PFTN·WJ-25、WH-20
爱尔兰共和国 Ireland	1979.6.22	PFTN·WJ-148、PFTN·WJ（C）-28
爱沙尼亚共和国 Republic of Estonia	1991.9.11	PFTN·WJ-74、PFTN·WJ2011-13
安道尔公国 The Principality of Andorra	1994.6.29	PFTN·WJ-150
奥地利共和国 The Republic of Austria	1971.5.28	PFTN·WJ-66、WH-8、WH-21、PFTN·WJ2011-5
白俄罗斯共和国 The Republic of Belarus	1992.1.20	PFTN·WJ-92、PFTN·WJ（C）-11、PFTN·WJ2012-7
保加利亚共和国 The Republic of Bulgaria	1949.10.4	PFTN·WJ-13、WH-14
比利时王国 The Kingdom of Belgium	1971.10.25	PFTN·WJ-80、PFTN·WJ2011-17
冰岛共和国 Republic of Iceland	1971.12.8	PFTN·WJ-84
波兰共和国 The Republic of Poland	1949.10.7	PFTN·WJ-21、WH-19
波斯尼亚和黑塞哥维那 Bosnia and Herzegovina	1995.4.3	PFTN·WJ-154、WH-24
大不列颠及北爱尔兰联合王国 The United Kingdom of Great Britain and Northern Ireland	1972.3.13	PFTN·WJ-101、PFTN·WJ2012-13
丹麦王国 The Kingdom of Denmark	1950.5.11	PFTN·WJ-35
德意志联邦共和国 The Federal Republic of Germany	1972.10.11	PFTN·WJ-116、PFTN·WJ-136、PFTN·WJ2012-32

中华人民共和国外交系列
特种纪念封　目录

国家	与中国建交日	外交纪念封编号（序号）
俄罗斯联邦 The Russian Federation	1949.10.2	PFTN·WJ-12、PFTN·WJ（B23）-173、WH-13、PFTN·WJ2011-9、WH-46
法兰西共和国 The Republic of France	1964.1.27	PFTN·WJ-2、PFTN·WJ（B9）-152
芬兰共和国 The Republic of Finland	1950.10.28	PFTN·WJ-53
荷兰王国 The Kingdom of the Netherlands	1972.5.18	PFTN·WJ2012-21
黑山 Montenegro	2006.7.6	PFTN·WJ2011-7
捷克共和国 The Czech Republic	1949.10.6	PFTN·WJ-19、WH-16
克罗地亚共和国 The Republic of Croatia	1992.5.13	PFTN·WJ-108、PFTN·WJ（C）-18、PFTN·WJ2012-20
拉脱维亚共和国 Republic of Latvia	1991.9.12	PFTN·WJ-75、PFTN·WJ2011-14
立陶宛共和国 The Republic of Lithuania	1991.9.14	PFTN·WJ-76、PFTN·WJ2011-15
列支敦士登公国 The Principality of Liechtenstein	1950.9.14	PFTN·WJ-47
卢森堡大公国 The Grand Duchy of Luxembourg	1972.11.16	PFTN·WJ-120、PFTN·WJ2012-33
罗马尼亚 Romania	1949.10.5	PFTN·WJ-15、WH-15
马耳他共和国 The Republic of Malta	1972.1.31	PFTN·WJ-95、PFTN·WJ2012-10
马其顿共和国 The Republic of Macedonia	1993.10.12	PFTN·WJ-137、PFTN·WJ（B19）-168、PFTN·WJ2013-7
摩尔多瓦共和国 The Republic of Moldova	1992.1.30	PFTN·WJ-94、PFTN·WJ（C）-12、PFTN·WJ2012-9
摩纳哥公国 The Principality of Monaco	1995.1.16	
挪威王国 The Kingdom of Norway	1954.10.5	PFTN·WJ-16
葡萄牙共和国 The Portuguese Republic	1979.2.8	PFTN·WJ-4、WH-1、WH-12
瑞典王国 The Kingdom of Sweden	1950.5.9	PFTN·WJ-34
瑞士联邦 Swiss Confederation	1950.9.14	PFTN·WJ-46
塞尔维亚共和国 The Republic of Serbia	1955.1.2	PFTN·WJ（B26）-178
塞浦路斯共和国 The Republic of Cyprus	1971.12.14	PFTN·WJ-85、PFTN·WJ（B16）-164、PFTN·WJ2011-21
圣马力诺共和国 The Republic of San Marino	1971.5.6	PFTN·WJ-64、PFTN·WJ2011-3
斯洛伐克共和国 The Slovak Republic	1949.10.6	PFTN·WJ-20、WH-17

218

国家	与中国建交日	外交纪念封编号（序号）
斯洛文尼亚共和国 The Republic of Slovenia	1992.5.12	PFTN·WJ-107、PFTN·WJ（C）-17、PFTN·WJ2012-19
乌克兰 Ukraine	1992.1.4	PFTN·WJ-88、PFTN·WJ（C）-7、PFTN·WJ2012-3、PFTN·WJ2013-11
西班牙王国 The Kingdom of Spain	1973.3.9	PFTN·WJ-129、PFTN·WJ（B18）-167、WH-59
希腊共和国 The Hellenic Republic	1972.6.5	PFTN·WJ-110、PFTN·WJ（C）-19、PFTN·WJ（B24）-174、PFTN·WJ2012-27、WH-45
匈牙利 Hungary	1949.10.6	PFTN·WJ-17、WH-18
意大利共和国 The Republic of Italy	1970.11.6	PFTN·WJ-55、WH-37、WH-38

四、北美洲 NORTH AMERICA

国家	与中国建交日	外交纪念封编号（序号）
安提瓜和巴布达 Antigua and Barbuda	1983.1.1	PFTN·WJ-125、WH-56
巴巴多斯 Barbados	1977.5.30	PFTN·WJ-109、PFTN·WJ2012-25
巴哈马国 The Commonwealth of the Bahamas	1997.5.23	PFTN·WJ2012-24
多米尼克国 The Commonwealth of Dominica	2004.3.23	
哥斯达黎加共和国 The Republic of Costa Rica	2007.6.1	PFTN·WJ-166、PFTN·WJ2012-26、WH-47
格林纳达 Grenada	1985.10.1	PFTN·WJ2010-2
古巴共和国 The Republic of Cuba	1960.9.28	PFTN·WJ-48、WH-33、PFTN·WJ2012-30
加拿大 Canada	1970.10.13	PFTN·WJ-51、WH-43、PFTN·WJ2013-8
美利坚合众国 The United States of America	1979.1.1	PFTN·WJ-1、PFTN·WJ-100、PFTN·WJ（C）-26、PFTN·WJ2011-20、WH-44
墨西哥合众国 The United Mexican States	1972.2.14	PFTN·WJ-98、PFTN·WJ2012-11
特立尼达和多巴哥共和国 The Republic of Trinidad and Tobago	1974.6.20	PFTN·WJ-9
牙买加 Jamaica	1972.11.21	PFTN·WJ-121、WH-53

五、南美洲 SOUTH AMERICA

国家	与中国建交日	外交纪念封编号（序号）
阿根廷共和国 Argentina Republic	1972.2.19	PFTN•WJ-99、PFTN•WJ（C）-13、PFTN•WJ2012-12
巴西联邦共和国 The Federative Republic of Brazil	1974.8.15	PFTN•WJ-11、PFTN•WJ2011-1
秘鲁共和国 The Republic of Peru	1971.11.2	PFTN•WJ-81、PFTN•WJ（C）-4、PFTN•WJ（B20）-170、PFTN•WJ2011-18、PFTN•WJ2013-1
多民族玻利维亚国 The Multinational States of Bolivia	1985.7.9	PFTN•WJ-42、PFTN•WJ2013-14
厄瓜多尔共和国 The Republic of Ecuador	1980.1.2	PFTN•WJ-26
哥伦比亚共和国 The Republic of Columbia	1980.2.7	PFTN•WJ-29、WH-22、PFTN•WJ2012-23
圭亚那共和国 The Republic of Guyana	1972.6.27	PFTN•WJ-112、PFTN•WJ2012-29
苏里南共和国 The Republic of Suriname	1976.5.28	PFTN•WJ-67、WH-9、PFTN•WJ2011-6
委内瑞拉玻利瓦尔共和国 The Bolivarian Republic of Venezuela	1974.6.28	PFTN•WJ-10、WH-2
乌拉圭东岸共和国 Oriental Republic of Uruguay	1988.2.3	PFTN•WJ-127、PFTN•WJ（C）-22、PFTN•WJ2013-2
智利共和国 Republic of Chile	1970.12.15	PFTN•WJ-58、PFTN•WJ（B21）-171、WH-39

六、大洋洲 OCEANIA

国家	与中国建交日	外交纪念封编号（序号）
澳大利亚联邦 The Commonwealth of Australia	1972.12.21	PFTN•WJ-122、PFTN•WJ2012-34
巴布亚新几内亚独立国 The Independent State of Papua New Guinea	1976.10.12	PFTN•WJ-79、PFTN•WJ（C）-3
斐济共和国 The Republic of Fiji	1975.11.5	PFTN•WJ-54
库克群岛 The Cook Islands	1997.7.25	
密克罗尼西亚 The Federated States of Micronesia	1989.9.11	PFTN•WJ-151、PFTN•WJ（C）-29
纽埃 Niue	2007.12.12	
萨摩亚独立国 The Independent State of Samoa	1975.11.6	PFTN•WJ-56

国家	与中国建交日	外交纪念封编号（序号）
汤加王国 The Kingdom of Tonga	1998.11.2	PFTN·WJ-139、PFTN·WJ（B22）-172、PFTN·WJ2013-9
瓦努阿图共和国 The Republic of Vanuatu	1982.3.26	PFTN·WJ-102、PFTN·WJ（C）-14、PFTN·WJ2012-14
新西兰 New Zealand	1972.12.22	PFTN·WJ-123、PFTN·WJ（C）-21、WH-55

七、国际组织（会议）International Organization and International Conference

国际组织（会议）	相关纪念日	外交纪念封编号（序号）
联合国 The United Nations	1971.10.25 恢复中华人民共和国合法席位	PFTN·WJ（B14）-162、PFTN·WJ（B25）-175
上海合作组织 The Shanghai Cooperation Organization	2001.6.15 成立日	PFTN·WJ（B13）-161
欧洲联盟 European Union	1975.5.6 建交日	PFTN·WJ-156、WH-27
东南亚国家联盟 Association of Southeast Asian Nations	1991.7.19 中国与东盟建立对话关系日	PFTN·WJ2011-10
中国阿拉伯友好协会 The Chinese-Arabic Friendship Association	2001.12.21 成立日	PFTN·WJ2011-22
和平解决朝鲜问题与恢复印度支那和平问题的日内瓦会议 The peaceful settlement of the Korean question and recovery of the Indochina peace conference in Geneva	1954.4.26 开幕日	PFTN·WJ（B6）-146
和平共处五项原则 The Five Principles of Peaceful Coexistence	1954.6.29	PFTN·WJ（B8）-149
万隆会议 Bandung Conference	2005.4.18-24	PFTN·WJ（B10）-155
中非合作论坛北京峰会 Beijing Summit of Forum on China-Africa Cooperation	2006.11.4-5	PFTN·WJ（B15）-163
第二次中日韩领导人会议 The Second Trilateral Summit Meeting among the People's Republic of China, Japan and the Republic of Korea	2009.10.10	PFTN·WJ（B27）-179
中国—中东欧国家合作秘书处 The Secretariat for Cooperation between China and Central and Eastern European Countries	2012.9.6 成立日	WH-49

后 记

经过数月的多次核对补充，外交系列特种纪念封目录即将付印。此时我们迎来了2014年元旦，正是1999年第一枚外交纪念封发行十五周年的日子。

十五年来，外交系列特种纪念封已经发行了三百多枚，涉及到一百六十五个国家和国际组织，其题材也不断拓展。外交系列特种纪念封已经成为中外友好交流的历史见证。

十五年来，每一种外交纪念封的发行，都是中外友好合作的结晶。一般先由外交部集邮协会、地区司和驻外使馆提出选题，纪念封的图案设计和说明文字需经外交部相关司局进行审核，并得到相关国家驻华使馆的确认。由于从确认到发行的时间有限，在外交纪念封的设计、制作和发行过程中，相关部门经常连夜突击赶工；纪念封需要发运到我国驻外使馆的，时间就更紧迫。有的驻华大使亲自为纪念封加盖邮戳，或亲笔签名。可以说，每一枚外交封都凝聚着中外人士为双方友谊付出的热情奉献。

在为外交纪念封发行举办的仪式上，大多有两国领导人或大使馆官员亲自出席，为纪念封揭幕，并签字留念，见证这历史的瞬间。

让中国更多地了解世界，让世界更多地了解中国。外交纪念封成为传递友好情谊的媒介，打开了一个相互了解的窗口。

外交纪念封的发行，吸引了众多集邮者。他们倾心收集、典藏、研究、展示外交纪念封不遗余力，成为外交纪念封的忠实"粉丝"。

作为外交系列特种纪念封的创意、策划和设计者，十五年来，我与外交封结下了不解之缘。看着这本目录样书，百感交集。五千多个日日夜夜，经常在部里和驻华使馆，以及印刷厂和机场之间奔波。而每每想到外交纪念封在外交人士和集邮者当中受到的欢迎，个中甘苦，一扫而光。

外交系列特种纪念封倾注了中外很多外交人士和集藏者的心血。借此机会，向所有为外交系列特种纪念封的发行和这本目录出版尽一己之力的中外友人表示衷心的感谢，致以崇高的敬意。

祝愿外交系列特种纪念封为增进中国人民与各国人民之间的友好合作不断做出新的贡献。

马小玲

2014 年 1 月

图书在版编目（CIP）数据

中华人民共和国外交系列特种纪念封目录 / 马小玲主编 .—北京：世界知识出版社，2013.9

ISBN 978-7-5012-4547-5

Ⅰ.① 中… Ⅱ.① 马… Ⅲ.① 邮票—目录—中国—1999～2013 ② 外交史—中国—现代 Ⅳ.① G894.1 ② D829

中国版本图书馆 CIP 数据核字（2013）第 224519 号

特约编辑	刘大有
责任编辑	车胜春
书　　名	中华人民共和国外交系列特种纪念封目录
主　　编	马小玲
出版发行	世界知识出版社
地址邮编	北京市东城区干面胡同 51 号（100010）
网　　址	www.wap1934.com
经　　销	新华书店
印　　刷	北京天工印刷有限公司
开本印张	787×1092 毫米　1/16　15 印张
字　　数	120 千字
版次印次	2014 年 3 月第一版　2014 年 3 月第一次印刷
标准书号	ISBN 978-7-5012-4547-5
定　　价	98.00 元

版权所有　侵权必究